I0796292

The
Unofficial
TikTok
Cookbook
VOLUME 2

Palestrina McCaffrey @littleremyfood

ADAMS MEDIA

NEW YORK AMSTERDAM/ANTWERP LONDON TORONTO SYDNEY/MELBOURNE NEW DELHI

For all the amazing content creators who made these viral recipes possible!

Adams Media
An Imprint of Simon & Schuster, LLC
100 Technology Center Drive
Stoughton, MA 02072

First Adams Media hardcover edition October 2025

ADAMS MEDIA and colophon are registered trademarks of Simon & Schuster, LLC.

The Unofficial TikTok Cookbook, Volume 2 is an independent publication and has not been authorized, sponsored, or otherwise approved by ByteDance Ltd.
TikTok is a registered trademark of ByteDance Ltd.

Interior design by Erin Alexander and Maya Caspi
Illustrations by Priscilla Yuen
Photographs by Harper Point Photography
Photography chefs: Kira Friedman and Martine English
Author photo by Marc Cartwright Photography

Manufactured in the United States of America

1 2025

Library of Congress Control Number: 2025941705

ISBN 978-1-5072-2432-8
ISBN 978-1-5072-2433-5 (ebook)

Always follow safety and commonsense cooking protocols while using kitchen utensils, operating ovens and stoves, and handling uncooked food. If children are assisting in the preparation of any recipe, they should always be supervised by an adult.

Acknowledgments

To my husband, Stephen: Thank you for always being my biggest supporter, producer, content editor, and expert dragon's beard puller.

To Cera and Jacob: Thank you for being willing guinea pigs and graciously accepting every "oops" batch of cookies and mystery treat that came out of this kitchen. Your friendship (and your tolerance for sugar) means the world.

To my indelible chemistry teacher, Teresa: Thank you for teaching me how to get curious and blow things up, and for believing in my passion for video when I was a kid.

To my fans: Thank you for all your love, comments, likes, and subscribes! You're the true reason I'm here, and I'm so grateful every day for each one of you who have followed me on this journey.

To the content creators who made this happen: Thank you for sharing your love in the kitchen, creating these viral recipes, and inspiring me to re-create them in mine.

Contents

Make It a Meal · 51

Bring It to a Party · 85

International Delights · 109

Sweet Treats · 137

Introduction

Smashburger Tacos . . . Flamin' Hot Cheetos Salad . . . Dubai Chocolate Bars loaded with creamy pistachio filling . . .

TikTok is full of creative and downright entertaining recipes that make us high-key *obsessed* with food. Whether it's the ultimate cheese pull via fried mozzarella, a satisfying crunch of Pizza Toast, or a perfectly imperfect drizzle of sweetened condensed milk on Hong Kong French Toast, you can practically taste the deliciousness through your For You page (FYP).

And now those tasty dishes can finally make it out of the group chat!

The *Unofficial TikTok Cookbook, Volume 2* is your VIP scoop on the Internet's greatest hits in the kitchen. From Honeycomb Candy and Dry Yogurt to Ramen Lasagna and Pull-Apart Holiday Cheese Bread, you'll find easy-to-make versions of seventy-five of the most viral dishes out there. Even better? You won't need fancy kitchen gadgets, culinary degrees, or a bunch of superpricey ingredients to make them!

Organized by chapter based on the type of dish, this cookbook has something for every vibe. Impress your friends with your flawless Tanghulu game for a late-night snack, fill up on a satisfying Chopped Italian Sandwich for lunch, or share a big dish of Million Dollar Spaghetti for dinner with the fam 🥰

You'll also find a chapter with tips for spotting other popular recipes that are worth trying, plus details for some tools and basic ingredients you'll want to keep on hand as you get cooking.

Whether you're a huge foodie, love a good trend, or just want to try something new, this book is here to help you master viral dishes one yummy ingredient at a time. So clear some space in the fridge, pull up those saved #FoodTok favorites, and let's cook!

CHAPTER 1

The Essentials of TikTok Cooking

TikTok is absolutely *stuffed* full of recipes. One second, you're drooling over perfectly golden Korean Corn Dogs, and with another swipe, you're mesmerized by a swirl of gooey Cinnamon Roll Donuts 🥰

But what lands some recipes on your FYP while others never seem to get views? And what things do you need to make these trending treats in your own kitchen? This chapter is here to clear things up!

You'll explore essential tools to simplify the process (hello, air fryer magic!), pantry staples to tackle any recipe, and the details on how to tell when a trending recipe is worth the hype—and when to skip it. Ready to dive in? Let's experiment with dishes inspired by TikTok's top hits!

#FoodTok

There used to be a time when a great recipe was a closely guarded family secret. Ever found yourself at a friend's house, amazed at how good their mom's cooking was? You probably heard something like, "It's a family recipe!" And that was that. But the age of gatekeeping food is over—thanks, TikTok! Now, sharing cooking tips and tricks and full recipes is easier than ever. We all get to experience the flavors, cultures, and creativity behind a tasty dish.

And when one person discovers a cool new way to make something, it catches on *fast*. Suddenly, everyone is trying it, adding their own spin, and sharing their reactions online. That collective "OMG, this is insane!" energy fuels the fun of food trends. The accessibility of these recipes, with simpler techniques and fewer ingredients, makes it easy for anyone to jump in, proving that good food doesn't have to be complicated. That's a big part of their charm! Most viral recipes are designed to be quick, fun, and beginner-friendly, and you don't need years of cooking experience to make something that looks and tastes amazing. The step-by-step visuals, short ingredient lists, and creative shortcuts strip away the pressure and make cooking feel simple. It all builds kitchen confidence, one trend at a time.

#Trending

But why do some foods go viral while others don't? Sometimes it's just plain curiosity. You scroll past a video of someone making a cucumber salad and think, "Oh, that looks good." Then another creator makes it. Then another. Then someone adds a twist—maybe a chili crisp drizzle or a crazy plating technique. Suddenly, you're asking yourself, "What am I missing??" That curiosity is what makes some recipes *so* irresistible.

But it's not just about repetition—it's about novelty too. A lot of viral recipes are things no one's ever seen before, like a dessert that melts when you pour milk on it, or a sandwich with rainbow bread. They're eye-catching, unexpected, and just wild enough to make you want to try them for yourself. Sometimes it's about breaking the rules of traditional cooking, and other times it's about remixing familiar favorites in a way that feels totally new. And of course, there's the shareability factor. If a recipe makes you say, "Wait, what?!" or laugh out loud, it's probably going to get reposted. The more it grabs your attention, the more likely it is to go viral.

Worth the Hype . . . or Not?

With so many viral recipes flooding your FYP, how do you know which ones are *actually* worth trying? Some trends take off because they're easy, delicious, and fun to make, while others blow up because they look good on camera but don't always translate to real life. The key is learning how to separate the game-changers from the overhyped. The magic of a recipe that's *worth* the hype isn't just in the taste—it's in the whole experience. These recipes are made to grab your attention, whether with a dramatic cheese pull, bright colors, or the satisfying crack of a caramel coating. Add in the reactions—someone taking a hesitant first bite, then *surprise*, it's 🔥 and you just have to try it yourself—and you're hooked!

When a recipe isn't worth your time, however, there's gonna be some red flags. Before you run to the kitchen, here's what to look at in those viral videos to know for sure:

- **Check the ingredients and steps involved.** Some viral recipes thrive on shock value. Suppose a recipe has a ton of steps, impossible-to-find ingredients, or a method that seems more like a stunt than actual cooking. In that case, it might not be worth your time.
- **Look at the reviews (and fails!).** One of the best parts of viral cooking culture is that people *love* sharing their results, good or bad. If a recipe has countless people raving about how easy and delicious it is, that's a great sign. But if you're seeing a flood of "Expectation vs. Reality" fails, you might want to think twice before attempting it yourself.
- **Ask yourself if you would actually make it again.** At the end of the day, the best test of a viral recipe is simple: Ask yourself, "Would I make this more than once?" The true winners aren't just fun for a one-time experiment—they earn a permanent place in your kitchen. If a recipe is something you'd happily whip up again and again, that's how you know it's a keeper.

Viral recipes can be unpredictable, but that's what makes them fun. So trust your instincts, experiment boldly, and don't be afraid to skip the trends that just don't seem worth it. When you find that *one* recipe that changes the game, that's when you'll get the hype. You can start out with some of the game-changers in this book, then check out other trends to try (or not try).

Essential Tools for Viral Cooking

TBH, viral food trends can make it seem like you need a high-tech kitchen straight from a sci-fi movie. The truth? Many of the most popular viral recipes thrive on creativity, clever techniques, and tools that pull double (or triple) duty—not complicated setups or impossible-to-find ingredients. Whether crisping air fryer nachos or whisking up the fluffiest pancakes, having a few versatile tools on hand makes all the difference. These real ✨ MVPs ✨ work across multiple trends, making cooking easier, faster, and, honestly, more fun!

They are:

- **Air fryer:** If there's one tool that's earned its Internet fame, it's the air fryer. Whether you're making juicy chicken bites or even baking a whole batch of brownies, this countertop wonder delivers a perfect crisp on the outside (*without* gallons of oil). Plus, it's a late-night-snack lifesaver—because who wants to preheat an oven for one serving of fries? It's perfect for re-creating recipes in this book like the take on TikTok-famous Pasta Chips, Air Fryer S'mores Dip, and the best cheesy Air Fryer Nachos! The recipes in this book are made with a 4-quart air fryer.
- **Candy thermometer:** If you've ever attempted Tanghulu, homemade caramel, or deep-fried desserts, you know that one wrong temperature reading can mean disaster. A candy thermometer ensures you hit the perfect sweet spot every time—no guesswork required. It's also crucial for making the trendy Honeycomb Candy and Dragon's Beard candy in this book . . . without burning everything to a crisp.
- **Stand or hand mixer:** Viral baking trends like Mochi Donuts and extra-fluffy pancakes often require whipping, kneading, or folding—all of which can be a serious arm workout! Save yourself some time and effort, and let a mixer handle the heavy lifting. Whether you're making ultra-light Macaron Croissants, perfectly Whipped Ricotta Toast, or elegant Japanese Fried Whipped Cream Sandwiches, a quality stand or hand mixer is your secret weapon.
- **Digital scale:** Outside of the US, most recipes are measured by weight rather than volume, which means a digital scale is essential if you want to

nail viral recipes from around the world. Whether you're making Japanese souffle pancakes or wondering why your mochi dough didn't turn out quite right, measuring by weight can be the difference between a recipe fail and a flawless final product.

- **Blowtorch:** Want that perfectly caramelized sugar crust on your crème brûlée? A blowtorch is your best friend. It's also a game-changer for torching cheese until it's bubbly and golden, crisping the top of viral s'mores dips, and adding a perfect charred finish to that Korean Marshmallow Ice Cream Bar 🤤 If you've ever envied the dramatic melted cheese pull in food videos, this tool is the key.
- **Piping bags and tips:** If you've ever been mesmerized by those beautifully piped viral cupcakes, perfectly stuffed cream puffs, or aesthetic Macaron Croissants, piping bags and tips are crucial. They're essential for precision when decorating cakes, filling donuts with gooey goodness, or even creating trendy Deviled Strawberries. This tool ensures every detail looks as good as it tastes!

Having these tools at the ready will help you re-create TikTok's biggest hits like a pro. You can also use them to experiment with your own tasty masterpieces—or to try out other recipes you've heard about.

Must-Have Pantry Staples

Before you turn on that mixer, you're gonna need some ingredients! No, you don't need an entire aisle's worth of spices to make great food—but a few essentials can level up just about any viral dish. Actually, many Internet-famous dishes use a mix of the same pantry staples. Keeping your kitchen stocked with these means you're always ready to whip up something tasty based on the latest TikTok sensation—whether it's Whipped Lemonade, S'mores Cookies, or Baked Feta Pasta.

First, you'll want to make sure you've got the starter pack:

- **Salt and pepper:** The foundation of literally everything.
- **Garlic powder and onion powder:** Perfect for seasoning viral pasta bakes and air-fried snacks.

- **Paprika and smoked paprika:** Essential for adding depth to trendy roasted potato dishes and crispy chicken. Smoked paprika is great for when you want to add a richer, smoky flavor, while regular paprika adds some kick.
- **Cinnamon:** From viral cinnamon roll pancakes to homemade churros, this one's a pantry hero.
- **Fresh and/or dried herbs:** Basil, cilantro, rosemary, and oregano can add more flavor and elevate everything from pesto pasta to a take on the TikTok-famous "Marry Me" Chicken Pasta. Most recipes in this book use fresh herbs, but dried can be used in smaller amounts (because they have a more concentrated flavor).

Then, once you've got the basics, it's time to move on to the real pantry MVPs:

- **All-purpose flour:** The key to desserts or deep-fried viral dishes like Korean Corn Dogs and Biscoff Nutella Brownies.
- **Cornstarch:** The not-so-secret ingredient behind Dragon's Beard and the extra-crispy fried chicken in Garlic Parmesan Chicken Tenders.
- **Granulated sugar and brown sugar:** Used in almost every trending dessert, from Mochi Donuts to crunchy Tanghulu.
- **Confectioners' sugar:** Essential for macarons, whipped cream, or Candied Cranberries.
- **Condensed milk:** A sweet game-changer for Whipped Lemonade or Hong Kong French Toast.
- **Soy sauce and rice vinegar:** Perfect for ramen hacks, sushi bakes, and viral sauces like the chili oil in Chili Oil Noodles.
- **Olive oil:** One of the most versatile ingredients, olive oil plays a key role in multiple recipes in this book, from crispy, crunchy Pasta Chips to the rich and creamy Lasagna Soup.
- **Neutral oil:** An oil with little to no flavor, like avocado oil or canola oil, gets you that golden-brown crust on fried chicken, Cinnamon Roll Donuts, or crispy Korean Corn Dogs.
- **Vanilla extract:** Almost every sweet viral recipe—from French Hot Chocolate to S'mores Cookies—uses a splash of this ingredient.

One of the best things about viral recipes is how creative they are: They take ordinary pantry staples like some flour and oil and turn them into something exciting. Whether you're inspired by TikTok's favorite butter board, experimenting with an ultra-crispy air fryer snack, or whipping up a gooey dessert, these ingredients are gonna be your secret weapons. Always make sure you're stocked up. Then, before you panic about needing a fancy ingredient list for a recipe, check your pantry. Chances are, you'll already have what you need to go viral in your own kitchen!

Bringing #FoodTok to Your Kitchen

Cooking shouldn't feel like a chore—or worse, a high-stakes science experiment. It's not about perfection; it's about creativity, discovery, and, most importantly, fun! Some recipes will surprise you with how easy and delicious they are. Others might not turn out quite as expected—but that's all part of the experience. Embrace the process, enjoy the learning curve, and keep experimenting.

The best part of viral cooking? You're never in it alone. Every recipe is a chance to connect—with the food *and* a community of other foodies all trying the same thing. If you're nailing a viral dish on the first try (or making a total mess 😋), you've got countless TikTokers just a screen away who can offer up tips or celebrate the win.

Up next are some of the Internet's most exciting, delicious, and just plain fun recipes for you to try. So grab your must-have tools and ingredients, and let's get cooking.

Because who knows? Your creation might just be TikTok's next big obsession.

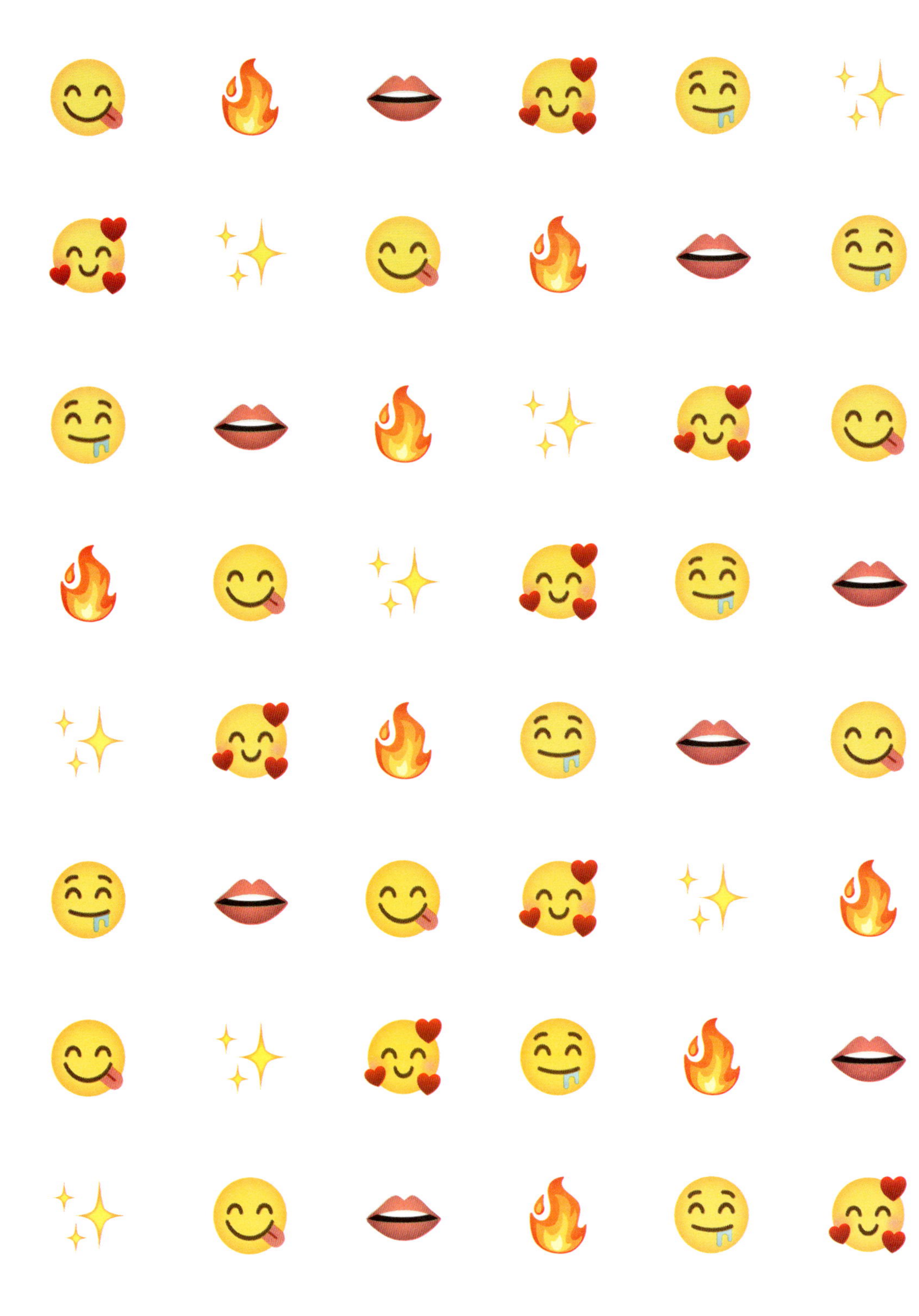

CHAPTER 2

Quick and Easy Bites

Cucumber Salad

Who knew something as simple as a cucumber would blow up online? This recipe proves that a humble veggie can be the star of the show, delivering crunch, flavor, and a refreshing bite in one takeout container. Let's just say, it's the perfect counterbalance to all those "girl dinner" nights!

SERVES 1

1 large English cucumber
2 teaspoons salt
1 tablespoon soy sauce
2 cloves garlic, peeled and minced
1 teaspoon minced fresh ginger
1 teaspoon sesame oil
2 tablespoons rice vinegar
1 tablespoon honey
1 teaspoon chili garlic sauce
½ teaspoon MSG
1 tablespoon sesame seeds

1. Using a mandoline or sharp knife, cut cucumber into very thin slices and place in a tall takeout-style container or medium bowl. Add salt, cover container, and shake to distribute salt evenly (or toss in a bowl). Set aside 5 minutes to draw out excess moisture. Drain, lightly rinse, and pat dry with paper towels.
2. Return cucumber slices to container or bowl and add soy sauce, garlic, ginger, oil, vinegar, honey, chili garlic sauce, and MSG. Toss until evenly coated.
3. Sprinkle with sesame seeds and serve immediately—or eat straight from the container for the full viral experience!

#ForYou Tips

Want to share this with some friends? Just scale up the ingredients and serve in a large bowl. This salad will disappear fast!

Cracked Latte

What's more satisfying than the sweet ASMR sounds of an iced latte? A ✨ CRACKED ✨ Latte, of course! This viral sensation combines the creamy, energizing goodness of an iced latte with a crunchy chocolate shell.

SERVES 1

2 (4-ounce) bars semisweet baking chocolate, roughly chopped

½ cup whole milk

1 tablespoon plus ¼ cup heavy cream, divided

1 tablespoon light brown sugar

¼ teaspoon vanilla extract

1 tablespoon instant coffee, hot chocolate mix, or matcha powder

1 tablespoon confectioners' sugar

1. Place chocolate in the top of a double boiler or a heatproof bowl set over a pan of simmering water. Stir constantly until melted, not exceeding 90°F. Pour melted chocolate into a 16-ounce flexible plastic cup and swirl to coat the inside of the cup. Freeze 3 minutes or until chocolate is solid.
2. In a separate large cup or mug, combine milk, 1 tablespoon cream, brown sugar, and vanilla. Whip with a frother or handheld blender until nice and creamy. Stir in coffee, hot chocolate mix, or matcha powder and whip or froth until incorporated.
3. In a small bowl, combine remaining ¼ cup cream and confectioners' sugar. Using an electric mixer set to medium-high speed or a whisk, beat about 3 minutes until soft peaks form.
4. Fill chocolate-lined cup with ice, and pour in your frothed drink. Top with whipped cream. Squeeze the cup to crack the chocolate shell and enjoy.

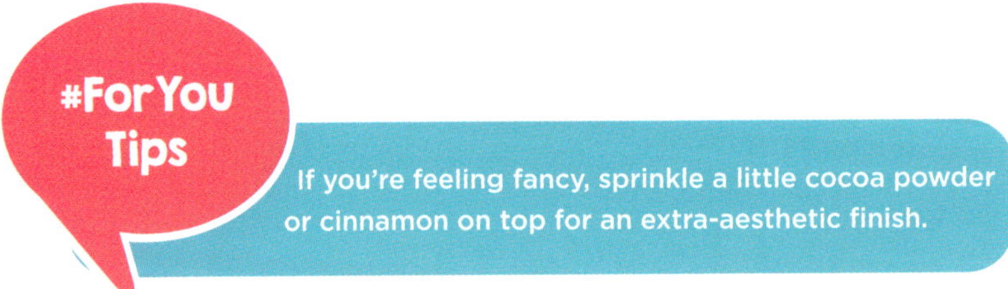

Carbonara Ramen

The Internet is packed with genius food hacks, but this Carbonara Ramen might just be one of the best. By taking instant ramen and giving it a creamy, cheesy, peppery upgrade, this dish is a next-level comfort meal. It's rich, smoky, and absolutely addictive—you'll be making it on repeat!

SERVES 1

1 tablespoon Kewpie mayonnaise

1 large egg yolk

¼ teaspoon cracked black pepper

2 teaspoons minced garlic

¼ cup plus 2 tablespoons grated Parmesan cheese, divided

1 (4.58-ounce) package uncooked Buldak carbonara flavor spicy chicken ramen, plus powder and hot sauce packets

2 slices uncooked bacon, finely chopped

1. In a small bowl, whisk together mayo, egg yolk, pepper, garlic, ¼ cup Parmesan, and Buldak carbonara powder packet from ramen package.
2. In a medium skillet over medium-high heat, add bacon. Cook and stir until crisp, about 3 minutes. Remove bacon with a slotted spoon and pour off grease. Return bacon to skillet.
3. Cook ramen noodles according to package instructions. Drain noodles, reserving cooking liquid. Place noodles in skillet and drizzle mayo mixture on top. Toss to combine, adding a tablespoon or two of cooking liquid if mixture is too thick.
4. Top with remaining 2 tablespoons Parmesan and Buldak hot sauce packet, toss, and enjoy!

Whipped Ricotta Toast

Fluffy, creamy, effortlessly elegant—Whipped Ricotta Toast is the glow up your breakfast *needs*. This viral trend turns plain ricotta cheese into a fresh and flavorful spread topped with tomatoes, honey, and herbs. It's a café-style brunch you can make in minutes!

SERVES 2

2 cups whole-milk ricotta cheese
1 teaspoon olive oil
¼ cup halved cherry tomatoes
1 teaspoon fresh thyme leaves
Salt
Ground black pepper
1 tablespoon honey
2 tablespoons unsalted butter
2 slices sourdough bread
½ teaspoon crushed red pepper flakes
1 teaspoon lemon juice
5 large fresh basil leaves, thinly sliced

1. Place ricotta in a cheesecloth-lined colander set over a bowl. Pull cheesecloth over ricotta and gently squeeze to remove excess liquid. Transfer ricotta to a medium bowl.
2. Using an electric mixer set to medium-high speed or a whisk, whip ricotta about 2 minutes until thick and creamy. Cover and refrigerate while you make the topping.
3. In a small skillet over medium heat, heat oil 30 seconds, then add tomatoes, thyme, salt, black pepper, and honey. Cook, stirring occasionally, about 10 minutes until tomatoes soften and caramelize.
4. In a medium skillet over medium-high heat, melt butter, then add bread slices. Toast until golden on both sides, about 2 minutes per side.
5. To assemble, pipe or spread whipped ricotta on toast. Sprinkle with red pepper flakes and drizzle with lemon juice. Top with tomato mixture and garnish with basil.

CANCEL
BAGEL
DEFROST

Dry Yogurt

Sometimes the simplest ingredient can become something unexpectedly luxurious. Dry Yogurt is proof of that. By taking out the excess moisture, yogurt turns into a thick, creamy treat with a texture so indulgent it feels like dessert 🤤 Topped with a drizzle of honey and some decadent chocolate, it's a game-changer for yogurt lovers everywhere!

SERVES 1

1 cup plain whole-milk Greek yogurt
1 tablespoon honey
¼ cup sliced strawberries
½ medium banana, peeled and sliced
1 ounce dark chocolate, chopped

1. Line a medium bowl with two layers of paper towels and scoop yogurt into the center. Fold paper towels over to completely wrap yogurt.
2. Refrigerate wrapped yogurt 24 hours to drain. After 12 hours, check the paper towels—if they're fully soaked, replace the outer layers with fresh ones to continue removing moisture.
3. After 24 hours, unwrap yogurt and transfer it to a small bowl. The texture should be thick, almost like cheesecake.
4. Drizzle with honey, then add strawberries and banana and top with chocolate.

Use a cheesecloth to remove even more liquid! You can leave it longer than 24 hours to get an even dryer consistency, or if you're using paper towels instead of a cheesecloth, change the paper towels every 4 hours to soak up more liquid.

Air Fryer Cinnamon Bagel

Sometimes you just need to satisfy those impulsive cravings. Enter the air fryer: your late-night snacking MVP. It's quick, it's easy, and it's here to turn your mid-night munchies into magic. After all, 1 a.m. snacks deserve to be iconic too. With the sweet hint of cinnamon, the creamy comfort of cream cheese, and a perfectly toasted crunch, this air fryer bagel is a hit that you'll want to create again and again.

SERVES 1

1 plain bagel, sliced horizontally
1 tablespoon unsalted butter, softened
¼ cup cream cheese, softened
2 tablespoons light brown sugar
1 teaspoon ground cinnamon

1. Preheat air fryer to 400°F.
2. Lightly toast bagel halves, then spread each with butter.
3. In a small bowl, mix together cream cheese, sugar, and cinnamon until smooth.
4. Spread cream cheese mixture generously over bagel halves, then place them in air fryer basket.
5. Air-fry 6–8 minutes until bagel halves are golden and the topping is bubbly.
6. Let cool 3–5 minutes before serving to ensure the topping sets and is safe to eat and enjoy.

Mix It Up

For an extra-indulgent twist, sprinkle a little confectioners' sugar or drizzle some honey on top before serving! You can also try different bagel flavors like cinnamon raisin or blueberry.

Pizza Toast

TBH, pizza cravings always seem to hit when cooking feels like waaaay too much effort. Enter Pizza Toast—the viral hack that brings all the cheesy, melty, crispy goodness of a slice of pizza without the hassle of making or cooking dough. It's quick, satisfying, and perfect for when you want homemade pizza *now*.

SERVES 1

1 tablespoon olive oil
2 slices French bread
4 tablespoons marinara sauce
½ cup grated Parmesan cheese, divided
4 slices fresh mozzarella cheese
8 pepperoni slices
⅛ teaspoon dried oregano
¼ teaspoon everything bagel seasoning
4 large fresh basil leaves, thinly sliced

1. Line air fryer basket with parchment paper (unless it is nonstick) and preheat to 385°F.
2. In a medium skillet over medium-high heat, heat oil 30 seconds. Add bread slices and toast until golden on both sides, about 2 minutes per side.
3. Spread marinara sauce evenly over both slices and sprinkle with ¼ cup Parmesan.
4. Add 2 slices mozzarella to each toast, then top with 4 slices pepperoni each. Sprinkle with remaining ¼ cup Parmesan.
5. Place toasts in air fryer basket and air-fry 8 minutes or until cheese is golden and bubbly.
6. Top with oregano, bagel seasoning, and basil. Serve immediately.

L.A.–Stuffed Cream Cheese Bagel

Some food trends are all about looks, but this L.A.-style stuffed bagel proves that flavor can match the aesthetic. With its buttery, garlicky crunch and creamy, cheesy filling, this favorite delivers an experience that's #newnominous. Every bite hits different, and once you try it, there's no going back to regular bagels!

SERVES 1–2

1 large plain bagel
½ cup whipped cream cheese
½ cup (1 stick) unsalted butter, melted
1 teaspoon minced garlic
2 tablespoons chopped fresh parsley
¼ cup shredded Parmesan cheese

1. Preheat oven or air fryer to 375°F.
2. Place bagel on a flat surface. Cut through the top into six equal sections, cutting about ⅔ of the way through—be careful not to cut all the way through.
3. Pipe or spread cream cheese into each cut.
4. In a medium bowl, combine butter, garlic, and parsley. Dunk bagel into mixture, turning to ensure it's fully coated in garlicky, buttery goodness.
5. Sprinkle Parmesan over the top. Transfer to a small ungreased baking sheet or the basket of an air fryer.
6. Bake or air-fry 8–10 minutes until bagel is golden and cheese is melted. Serve immediately.

ALL NATURAL
ORANGE
JUICE

Frozen Jell-O Grapes

The Internet can't get enough of these frosty, flavor-packed grapes, and for good reason! Coated in tangy Jell-O powder and frozen to perfection, they're like a cross between sour candy and an ice-cold treat. Easy to make, ridiculously refreshing, and totally addictive—you'll wanna keep a stash of these in your freezer at all times.

SERVES 4

¼ cup lime juice
1 (3-ounce) packet cherry-flavored gelatin mix
1 (3-ounce) packet blue raspberry-flavored gelatin mix
1 (3-ounce) packet lime-flavored gelatin mix
2 cups white or cotton candy grapes

1. Line a large baking sheet with parchment paper.
2. Pour lime juice into a small bowl. Pour gelatin mixes into three separate small bowls.
3. Using a toothpick, skewer a grape, dip it into lime juice, then sprinkle with one of the gelatin mix flavors using a spoon. Place on prepared baking sheet. Repeat with remaining grapes, alternating flavors.
4. Place baking sheet in freezer and freeze at least 4 hours or until fully frozen.
5. Remove from freezer, transfer grapes to a serving bowl, and enjoy! Grapes can be stored in the freezer up to 3 days in an airtight container.

Egg-in-a-Hole Toast

Why have eggs and toast separately, when you can combine them into the ultimate all-in-one bite? This simple, nostalgic breakfast is popular for a reason: It's quick, filling, and delicious. Whether you're making it for the aesthetic or just craving a perfectly runny yolk, this classic dish is a tasty way to start the day!

SERVES 1

1 slice white bread
1 tablespoon unsalted butter
1 large egg
Salt
Ground black pepper
Crushed red pepper flakes
Nutella hazelnut spread (optional)

1. Using the rim of a glass, press firmly into the center of the bread to cut out a circle. Set the cutout aside.
2. In a medium skillet over medium-high heat, melt butter. Swirl pan to coat the bottom.
3. Place bread in skillet and toast about 1 minute until golden on the bottom. Flip, then crack egg into the hole in the center.
4. Cook 1–2 minutes until egg white begins to set. Season with salt and black pepper, then carefully flip and cook another 45 seconds or until egg white is fully cooked through.
5. Remove from heat and sprinkle with red pepper flakes.
6. If you like, toast the reserved bread cutout and spread with Nutella.

Soup in a Jar

When you've only got 5 minutes to make a meal, but you're still craving something warm and satisfying, Soup in a Jar is a perfect solution. This viral meal-prep hack is quick, balanced, and eliminates the need for dishes—just add hot water, shake, and go. It's perfect for a grab-and-go lunch or a cozy, effortless meal 🥰

SERVES 1

¼ chicken bouillon cube

¼ cup shredded rotisserie chicken

1¾ ounces (50g) uncooked vermicelli noodles

¼ cup frozen mixed vegetables

1 tablespoon miso paste

½ teaspoon minced fresh ginger

2 teaspoons soy sauce

1 teaspoon sesame oil

1 cup hot water

Sriracha

1. In a 16-ounce Mason jar, layer bouillon, chicken, noodles, vegetables, miso paste, ginger, soy sauce, and oil.
2. If making immediately, pour hot water into the jar, close it tightly, and shake gently until the ingredients are well combined. Let sit 2–4 minutes to allow the flavors to meld.
3. For meal prep, cover jar and refrigerate up to 4 days. When ready to make, remove jar from the refrigerator and set aside 10–20 minutes. (Hot water poured into a cold glass jar may cause it to crack.) Then add hot water and stir.
4. Top with sriracha and serve immediately.

For an extra protein boost, heat up some frozen chicken or pork dumplings following the package instructions and mix them in when the soup is ready to eat!

Cheese-Wrapped Pickles (Chickles)

Crispy, cheesy, salty, and just a *liiiitle* bit sour, this viral snack is the ultimate flavor bomb. Chickles combine a golden, crunchy cheese shell with a tangy pickle in the center for a quick-fix treat that's pretty much impossible to resist.

SERVES 1

2 slices extra-sharp Cheddar cheese
2 pickle spears
1 teaspoon garlic powder
2 tablespoons ranch dressing

1. Spray a medium nonstick skillet with cooking spray and place over medium-low heat. Place both cheese slices in skillet and let them melt and bubble slightly, about 30 seconds.
2. Reduce heat to low and place a pickle spear on top of each cheese slice.
3. Sprinkle with garlic powder and let cheese cook 1–2 minutes until the bottom is golden brown and crispy.
4. Using a spatula, carefully fold cheese over pickle until fully wrapped, then remove from heat. Serve immediately with ranch dressing for dipping.

Cucumber Roll-Ups

Lunch just got a serious upgrade! These Cucumber Roll-Ups deliver the perfect combo of crunch, creaminess, and bold flavors—all in a bite-sized 'lil package. Add more heat with a drizzle of sriracha mayo on top.

SERVES 1

1 large English cucumber

2 tablespoons cream cheese, softened

Salt

Ground black pepper

¼ teaspoon crushed red pepper flakes

½ (5-ounce) can water-packed tuna, drained

1 teaspoon onion powder

1 teaspoon garlic powder

½ teaspoon smoked paprika

1½ tablespoons Kewpie mayonnaise, divided

¼ medium avocado, peeled, pitted, and thinly sliced

1 tablespoon sriracha

1. Place a layer of plastic wrap on a flat cutting board.
2. Use a vegetable peeler to carefully slice cucumber into thin, vertical strips and lay them flat on the plastic wrap in an 8″ × 8″ square, slightly overlapping in a crisscross pattern to hold together.
3. Spread a thin layer of cream cheese over half of the cucumber surface. Sprinkle with salt, black pepper, and red pepper flakes.
4. In a small bowl, mix tuna, onion powder, garlic powder, smoked paprika, and ½ tablespoon mayonnaise until well combined. Spread tuna mixture evenly over cream cheese. Top with avocado slices.
5. Using the plastic wrap, carefully roll tightly from the filled end, pressing gently to secure the roll.
6. Secure the roll with toothpicks about an inch apart. Use a serrated knife to slice between the toothpicks to make bite-sized pieces.
7. In a small bowl, combine sriracha and remaining 1 tablespoon mayonnaise. Drizzle over roll-ups and enjoy!

Shaved Fruit

On those hot days when the AC's cranking and you're craving something cold, sweet, and refreshing, Shaved Fruit is the ultimate viral hack. This melt-in-your-mouth treat is like nature's version of shaved ice—no fancy machines required. The best part? It's *endlessly* customizable. Pick your favorite fruit, shave it down, and drizzle it with a sweet, tangy finish. Just be warned: It melts fast, so don't wait too long to dig in!

SERVES 1

1 large mango, peeled, pitted, and cut into large pieces (or your favorite fruit)
1 tablespoon lime juice
1 tablespoon honey

1. Line a small baking sheet with parchment paper.
2. Arrange mango on prepared baking sheet. Freeze overnight.
3. Using a cheese grater or the grater attachment on a stand mixer, shave frozen fruit into delicate, icy flakes. Scoop into a small bowl or glass.
4. Drizzle with lime juice and honey for a perfect balance of sweetness and tang. Serve immediately.

Feta Fried Egg

Short on time and want something crispy and satisfying ASAP? This Feta Fried Egg is truly the GOAT—crispy, golden feta and a perfectly runny yolk layered onto creamy avocado and a warm tortilla. This quick, trending recipe packs every possible flavor and texture into one single bite. You'll never wanna make eggs any other way again.

SERVES 1

½ cup crumbled feta cheese
1 large egg
Salt
Ground black pepper
¼ teaspoon crushed red pepper flakes
1 (6") flour tortilla
½ medium avocado, peeled, pitted, and mashed
1 tablespoon lime juice
2 teaspoons chopped fresh chives

1. Spray a medium nonstick skillet with cooking spray and place over medium-high heat.
2. Sprinkle feta evenly in prepared skillet to cover the bottom. Allow feta to sizzle about 1 minute until crisp and golden.
3. Carefully crack egg over crispy feta. Season with salt, pepper, and red pepper flakes. Cook 2–3 minutes until egg whites are set but yolk remains runny.
4. While egg cooks, place tortilla in a small skillet over medium heat. Toast until lightly golden on both sides, about 2 minutes per side.
5. Remove tortilla from heat and spread avocado on top. Drizzle with lime juice.
6. Place crispy Feta Fried Egg onto avocado-topped tortilla. Garnish with chives and serve immediately.

Grated Egg Avocado Toast

Grated eggs are the perfect breakfast hack. This trending method ensures every bite is fluffy, flavorful, and beautifully balanced—thanks, TikTok! Pair the eggs with creamy avocado and crunchy toast in this recipe, and you've got an effortlessly delicious upgrade that's as aesthetic as it is tasty.

SERVES 1

2 large eggs
1 tablespoon olive oil
2 slices sourdough bread
½ medium avocado, peeled, pitted, and thinly sliced
Salt
Ground black pepper
2 teaspoons everything bagel seasoning
2 teaspoons honey
½ teaspoon crushed red pepper flakes

1. Bring a small saucepan of water to a boil over high heat (make sure eggs are completely submerged in water). Add eggs and cook 10 minutes. Immediately transfer to an ice bath, let cool 2–3 minutes, then peel.
2. Using a fine grater, grate eggs into a small bowl and set aside.
3. In a medium skillet over medium heat, heat oil 30 seconds. Add bread slices and toast until golden on both sides, about 2 minutes per side.
4. Arrange avocado slices evenly on toasted bread and season with salt and pepper.
5. Top avocado toast with grated egg, sprinkle with bagel seasoning, drizzle with honey, and finish with red pepper flakes.

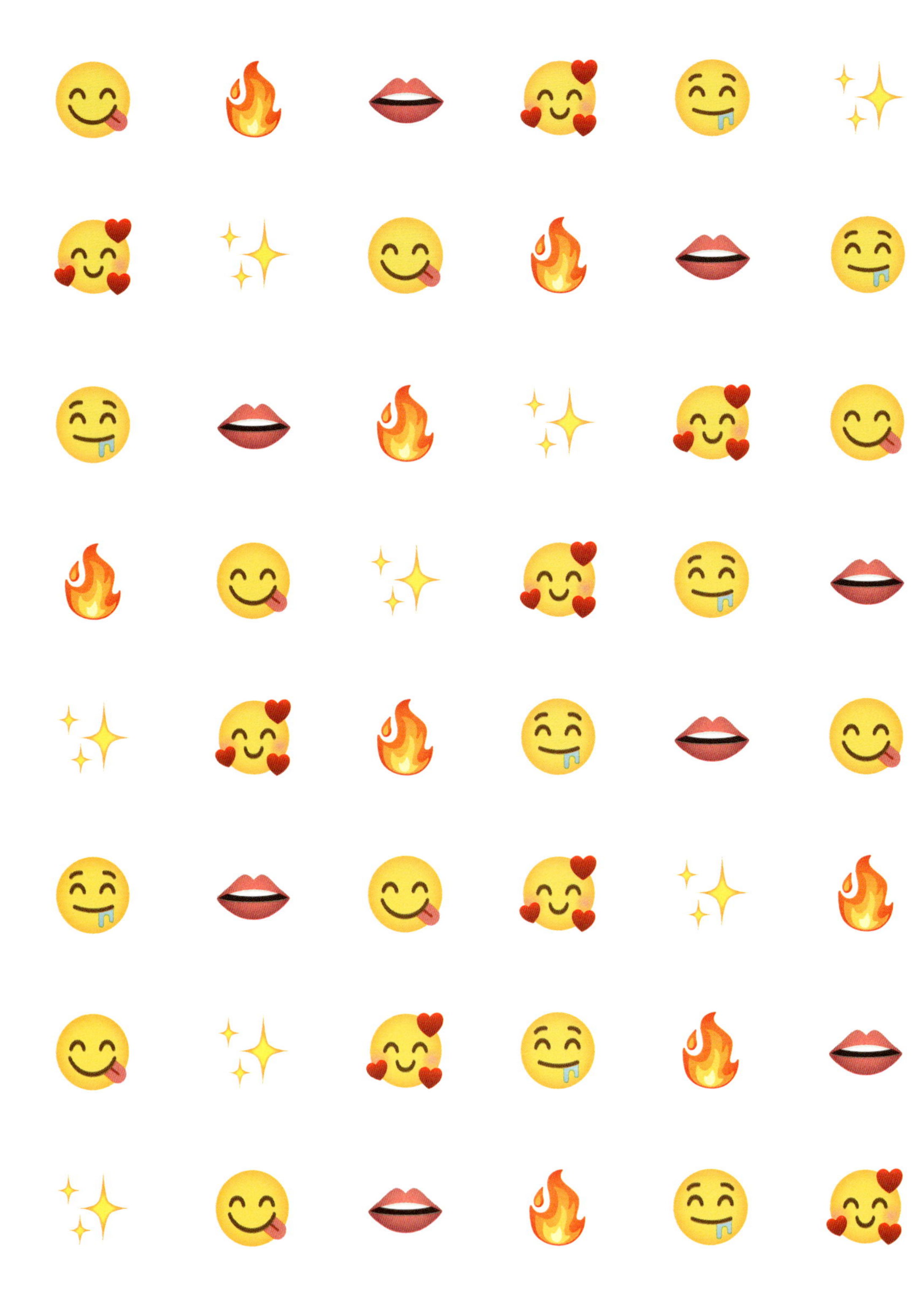

CHAPTER 3

Make It a Meal

Chopped Italian Sandwich

Why does chopping up a sandwich filling before putting it on bread make such a difference? No one's really sure, but it does! Every bite is perfectly balanced with the salty kick of cured meats, the crunch of fresh veggies, and the creamy touch of mayo. Inspired by the recipe that took TikTok by storm for a reason—it's a simple yet game-changing way to level up your lunch. Say goodbye to boring desk sandwiches forever.

SERVES 1

2 slices provolone cheese
3 slices deli ham
3 slices Genoa salami
3 large slices pepperoni
¼ cup shredded lettuce
2 slices tomato, diced
2 tablespoons diced red onion
2 tablespoons chopped banana pepper
1 tablespoon mayonnaise
1 teaspoon olive oil
1 teaspoon red wine vinegar
Salt
Ground black pepper
1 hoagie roll, split

1. On a cutting board, combine cheese, ham, salami, pepperoni, lettuce, tomato, onion, and banana pepper. Chop everything together until finely diced and fully mixed.
2. In a small bowl, stir together mayonnaise, oil, vinegar, salt, and black pepper. Drizzle over chopped mixture and toss until evenly coated.
3. Scoop the filling onto the hoagie roll, pressing lightly to ensure it stays in place.
4. Serve immediately and enjoy!

Smashburgers

Smashing down burger patties might just be the best food trend the Internet's given us. Thin, crispy edges; juicy centers; and stacked layers mean every bite is *packed* with maximum flavor 😋

SERVES 4

¼ cup mayonnaise
½ tablespoon ketchup
½ tablespoon mustard
1 teaspoon smoked paprika
¼ teaspoon cayenne pepper
1½ pounds 80% lean ground beef
1 teaspoon onion powder
1 teaspoon garlic powder
½ teaspoon ground black pepper
½ teaspoon salt
1 tablespoon unsalted butter
4 hamburger buns, sliced
8 slices American cheese
½ cup shredded lettuce
½ medium yellow onion, peeled and thinly sliced
12 dill pickle slices

1. Prepare the special sauce in a small bowl: Stir together mayonnaise, ketchup, mustard, smoked paprika, and cayenne pepper. Set aside.
2. In a large bowl, combine beef, onion powder, garlic powder, black pepper, and salt. Mix gently until just combined.
3. Form beef mixture into eight palm-sized balls (about 3 ounces each) and set aside on a large baking sheet lined with parchment paper.
4. In a large skillet over medium heat, melt butter. Add buns, cut side down, and toast 1–2 minutes until golden. Remove buns from skillet and set aside.
5. Increase heat to high and place beef balls onto the hot skillet. Using a spatula or patty press, firmly smash patties thin. Cook 1–2 minutes until crispy, flip once, and immediately top each with 1 slice cheese. Cook another 30–45 seconds until cheese melts.
6. Spread special sauce generously on top buns. Layer lettuce, onion, pickles, and two smash patties on bottom buns. Close buns and enjoy!

Ratatouille

OG Ratatouille has taken its viral spot thanks to warm, rich tomato juices and a delicate herbal flavor. It might sound superfancy, but this recipe is actually really simple—and looks *stunning*. Sometimes the simplest things in life really are the best.

SERVES 6–8

1 medium red bell pepper, seeded and quartered

2 medium shallots, peeled and halved

1 head garlic, cloves separated and peeled

1 medium jalapeño pepper, seeded and halved

2 large heirloom tomatoes, cut into wedges

2 tablespoons olive oil

2½ teaspoons salt, divided

2½ teaspoons ground black pepper, divided

2 small Japanese eggplants, thinly sliced

2 medium zucchini, thinly sliced

2 medium summer squash, thinly sliced

4 medium Roma tomatoes, thinly sliced

¼ teaspoon crushed red pepper flakes

2 teaspoons fresh thyme leaves

1 tablespoon chopped fresh basil

1. Preheat oven to 425°F.
2. Place bell pepper, shallots, garlic, jalapeño, and heirloom tomatoes on a large ungreased baking sheet and spread out evenly. Drizzle with oil, then season with 2 teaspoons each salt and black pepper. Roast 45 minutes.
3. Remove from oven. Carefully transfer roasted vegetables to a blender. Blend 2 minutes at high speed until smooth to create the sauce. Leave the oven on.
4. Pour sauce onto the bottom of a lightly greased 10″ oven-safe skillet or round baking dish.
5. Arrange vegetable slices upright over the sauce, alternating eggplant, zucchini, summer squash, and Roma tomato in a spiral pattern from the outer edge toward the center until skillet is full. Bake 45 minutes or until vegetables are tender and lightly caramelized.
6. Remove from oven and sprinkle with red pepper flakes, thyme, basil, and remaining ½ teaspoon each salt and black pepper. Serve warm and enjoy!

Lasagna Soup

One-pot meals are the ultimate dinner hack, and this hearty, comforting soup has all the flavors of OG lasagna—without the time-consuming layering. It's cozy, satisfying, and perfect for when you want something quick and delicious. So grab a spoon and snap that pasta: Lasagna just got *waaay* easier!

SERVES 6

1 tablespoon olive oil
1 medium yellow onion, peeled and chopped
1 pound 85% lean ground beef
1 pound ground Italian sausage
3 cloves garlic, peeled and minced
1 teaspoon salt
½ teaspoon ground black pepper
1 teaspoon dried oregano
1 teaspoon dried parsley
1 teaspoon Italian seasoning
1 (24-ounce) jar marinara sauce
3 cups chicken broth
½ cup heavy cream
8 uncooked lasagna noodles, broken into pieces
½ cup grated Parmesan cheese
1 cup shredded mozzarella cheese
¼ cup chopped fresh basil

1. In a large soup pot over medium heat, heat oil 30 seconds. Add onion and sauté 3–4 minutes until softened.
2. Add beef and sausage. Cook, breaking up the meat with a wooden spoon, until browned, about 5 minutes. Stir in garlic, salt, pepper, oregano, parsley, and Italian seasoning.
3. Pour in marinara sauce, broth, and cream. Stir to combine and increase heat to medium-high. Bring just to a boil, then reduce heat to medium-low. Simmer 20 minutes, stirring occasionally.
4. Add noodles to the pot and continue simmering until noodles are al dente, about 10 minutes.
5. Stir in Parmesan and mozzarella cheeses, allowing them to melt into the soup.
6. Garnish with basil and serve hot.

Baked Feta Pasta

Need a quick, foolproof meal? This take on a TikTok classic is *it*. The creamy feta melts into a rich, cheesy sauce while the roasted tomatoes burst with tangy flavor, creating the easiest pasta upgrade you'll ever make. Whether it's a last-minute dinner or a grocery store run turned gourmet, this dish is a guaranteed win.

SERVES 6

2 pints (20 ounces) cherry tomatoes
1 medium shallot, peeled and minced
2 tablespoons olive oil
Salt
Ground black pepper
1 (8-ounce) block feta cheese
½ pound uncooked cavatappi pasta
4 cloves garlic, peeled and minced
¼ cup chopped fresh basil

1. Preheat oven to 400°F.
2. Lightly grease a 9" × 13" baking dish and add tomatoes, shallot, oil, salt, and pepper. Stir gently.
3. Place feta in the center of the dish, surrounded by tomato mixture, then bake 40 minutes or until tomatoes are blistered and feta is soft.
4. While cheese bakes, cook pasta according to package instructions until al dente, then drain and set aside.
5. Using a fork, carefully poke and mash roasted tomatoes to release their juices. Stir tomatoes into the softened feta to form a sauce. Stir in garlic and basil.
6. Add cooked pasta to the baking dish and mix until fully coated in the creamy sauce. Serve immediately.

Nashville Hot Chicken Sandwiches

The Internet lost its absolute mind over Nashville hot chicken sandwiches, and it's not a surprise. With their irresistibly crispy coating and fiery flavor, these sandwiches deliver a perfect balance of crunchy, juicy, and spicy in every bite—capturing the vibrant heat of the South right in your kitchen 🔥 Paired with smoky mayo and tangy pickles, this version deserves TikTok fame!

SERVES 4

Smoky Mayo Sauce

½ cup mayonnaise
¼ cup ketchup
2 tablespoons diced dill pickle
2 teaspoons smoked paprika
½ teaspoon garlic powder
1 teaspoon salt
1 teaspoon ground black pepper

Chicken and Marinade

1 cup buttermilk
½ cup Frank's RedHot sauce
2 tablespoons dill pickle juice
2 teaspoons ground cayenne pepper
½ teaspoon smoked paprika
1 teaspoon salt
1 teaspoon ground black pepper
4 (5-ounce) boneless, skinless chicken thighs
2 large eggs
6 cups canola oil

Dry Batter

1½ cups all-purpose flour
½ cup cornstarch
1 teaspoon baking powder
1 teaspoon ground cayenne pepper
1 teaspoon ground black pepper
½ teaspoon smoked paprika

Hot Oil Sauce

1 tablespoon light brown sugar
½ teaspoon paprika
1 teaspoon ground cayenne pepper
1 teaspoon chili powder
1 teaspoon garlic powder
1 teaspoon salt
½ teaspoon ground black pepper

Assembly

2 tablespoons unsalted butter
4 brioche buns, sliced
12 dill pickle slices

Continued

Smoky Mayo Sauce

In a small bowl, combine mayonnaise, ketchup, diced pickle, smoked paprika, garlic powder, salt, and black pepper. Stir until smooth, then refrigerate until ready to assemble sandwiches.

Chicken and Marinade

1. In a large bowl, whisk together buttermilk, hot sauce, pickle juice, cayenne pepper, smoked paprika, salt, and black pepper until combined. Add chicken thighs and stir to ensure they're fully submerged. Cover with plastic wrap and refrigerate at least 2 hours, preferably overnight.
2. Remove chicken from marinade and place on a wire rack. Add eggs to marinade and whisk until smooth.
3. Heat oil in a large, deep pot over medium-high heat until it reaches 350°F.

Dry Batter

1. In a shallow dish, combine flour, cornstarch, baking powder, cayenne pepper, black pepper, and smoked paprika.
2. Working with one piece at a time, dredge chicken in flour mixture, coating evenly. Then dip in buttermilk and egg mixture and again in flour mixture for a second coating. Place chicken on the wire rack to rest 15 minutes.
3. Before frying, carefully reserve ½ cup hot oil and set aside.
4. Gently lower chicken thighs into the hot oil, frying in batches (1 or 2 pieces at a time) to maintain oil temperature. Fry each piece 8–10 minutes, flipping occasionally, until golden brown and fully cooked through. Maintain oil temperature between 325°F–350°F.
5. Immediately after frying, place chicken on a clean wire rack.

Hot Oil Sauce

In a small bowl, whisk reserved ½ cup hot oil with sugar, paprika, cayenne pepper, chili powder, garlic powder, salt, and black pepper until fully combined. Brush hot oil sauce over each piece of chicken using a silicone brush.

Assembly

In a medium skillet over medium-high heat, melt butter. Add buns, cut side down, and toast 1–2 minutes until golden. Spread about 1 tablespoon Smoky Mayo Sauce onto a top bun. Place a fried chicken piece and 3 pickle slices on a bottom bun. Close sandwich, repeat with remaining ingredients, and serve immediately.

#ForYou Tips

Use a digital thermometer to ensure the chicken is completely cooked in the center. The thermometer should read at least 165°F when ready.

Folded Tortilla Wraps

Who knew that a little folding trick could take wraps to the next level? This viral method keeps all the layers intact, perfectly balanced, and mess-free—no rolling, flipping, or overstuffing disasters. Just crispy, melty, flavor-packed perfection in every bite 🤤 Once you've mastered the fold, swap out ingredients for different flavor combos—go savory, sweet, or anything in between!

SERVES 2

1 teaspoon garlic powder
1 teaspoon onion powder
2 teaspoons paprika
½ teaspoon salt
½ teaspoon ground black pepper
1 tablespoon plus 1 teaspoon olive oil, divided
1 (7-ounce) boneless, skinless chicken breast, pounded slightly
1 tablespoon mayonnaise
2 teaspoons barbecue sauce
2 (10") burrito-sized tortillas
½ cup shredded lettuce
4 thin slices beefsteak tomato
½ cup shredded mozzarella cheese
½ cup shredded pepper jack cheese

1. Line air fryer basket with parchment paper (unless it is nonstick) and preheat to 375°F.
2. In a small bowl, mix together garlic powder, onion powder, paprika, salt, and pepper. Brush both sides of chicken with 1 tablespoon oil and season with garlic powder mixture. Place chicken in air fryer basket.
3. Air-fry 20 minutes, flipping halfway through. Use a meat thermometer to ensure the internal temperature reaches 165°F. Remove from air fryer and transfer to a cutting board. Let rest 1 minute, then slice diagonally into strips.
4. In a small bowl, combine mayonnaise and barbecue sauce.
5. Place tortillas on a flat surface and cut a slit halfway up the center of each.

Continued

Continued

6. Visually divide the tortillas into four quadrants. Place the ingredients in the quadrants as listed here:
   Bottom left: Chicken slices
   Top left: Mayonnaise mixture
   Top right: Lettuce and tomato
   Bottom right: Cheeses
7. In a clockwise formation, fold the tortillas: Starting with the bottom left corner, fold it over the top left, then fold to the top right, and finally to the bottom right to create a compact, layered wrap.
8. Brush a medium skillet with remaining 1 teaspoon oil and place over medium heat. Place folded wraps in skillet and cook each side 3 minutes, pressing down gently to flatten and ensure even crisping.
9. Serve hot and enjoy!

#ForYou Tips

No air fryer? Shred up a cooked rotisserie chicken instead for an even quicker version!

Ramen Lasagna

One of the best things about the Internet? The food combos you might never think of! A twist on classic ramen and lasagna, this recipe layers ramen noodles with cheesy, Italian-inspired goodness. Quick, comforting, and deliciously unexpected, it's perfect for an easy dinner that tastes way more indulgent than it should.

SERVES 6–8

6 (3-ounce) packages uncooked ramen
1½ cups whole-milk ricotta cheese
1 (32-ounce) jar marinara sauce
1½ cups heavy whipping cream
24 slices pepperoni
2 cups shredded mozzarella cheese
1 tablespoon Italian seasoning
1 teaspoon ground black pepper

1. Preheat oven to 350°F and lightly grease a 9″ × 13″ baking dish.
2. Place uncooked ramen noodles in a single layer across the bottom of the dish. Sprinkle noodles evenly with 3 ramen seasoning packets. Discard remaining packets or reserve for another use.
3. Spread ricotta over noodles. Pour marinara sauce and cream over the ricotta layer.
4. Arrange pepperoni slices across the dish, then top with mozzarella. Sprinkle with Italian seasoning and pepper.
5. Bake uncovered 50 minutes or until bubbly and golden brown.
6. Remove from oven, let rest briefly, and serve hot.

"Marry Me" Chicken Pasta

Rich, creamy, and restaurant-level good, this recipe's apparently got people popping the question! It turns a simple weeknight dinner into a whole vibe.

SERVES 6–8

1 pound uncooked bow tie pasta

1½ pounds boneless, skinless chicken breast, cut into 1″ cubes

2 teaspoons smoked paprika, divided

2 teaspoons onion powder, divided

2 teaspoons garlic powder, divided

2 teaspoons salt, divided

2 teaspoons ground black pepper, divided

2 tablespoons olive oil, divided

1 medium yellow onion, peeled and diced

6 cloves garlic, peeled and minced

½ (6-ounce) can tomato paste

2 ounces (about 1 cup) sun-dried tomatoes, chopped

1 teaspoon dried oregano

½ teaspoon crushed red pepper flakes

1½ cups chicken stock

1 cup heavy cream

1 cup grated Parmesan cheese

1 cup shredded mozzarella cheese

½ cup chopped fresh parsley

½ cup chopped fresh basil

1. Cook pasta according to package instructions. Drain and set aside. In a large bowl, toss chicken with 1 teaspoon each smoked paprika, onion powder, garlic powder, salt, and black pepper until evenly coated.
2. In a large, deep frying pan over medium heat, heat 1 tablespoon oil 30 seconds. Add chicken and stir-fry 8–10 minutes until fully cooked. Remove from pan and set aside.
3. Add remaining 1 tablespoon oil to pan. Sauté onion and garlic 5–6 minutes until translucent. Stir in tomato paste, sun-dried tomatoes, oregano, and red pepper flakes. Add stock, cream, and remaining 1 teaspoon each smoked paprika, onion powder, garlic powder, salt, and black pepper. Increase heat to medium-high and bring to a boil, then reduce heat to medium.
4. Add chicken and pasta to pan, stirring well to coat everything in the sauce. Simmer about 5 minutes until heated through. Stir in Parmesan, mozzarella, parsley, and basil. Mix until the cheeses melt. Enjoy!

Salmon and Rice Bowls

The salmon rice bowl craze created TikTok #foodheaven, and for good reason. This quick, delicious meal blends the perfect mix of flavors, giving you the taste of sushi—but way faster. In this version, the salmon is cooked up easily in the air fryer. Top it off with fresh avocado, crisp seaweed, and a drizzle of sriracha, and you've got a meal worth the hype.

SERVES 1

½ cup cooked white or brown rice
1 (5-ounce) skinless salmon fillet
1 tablespoon Kewpie mayonnaise
1 tablespoon soy sauce
Salt
Ground black pepper
½ medium avocado, peeled, pitted, and sliced
½ tablespoon sriracha
4 snack-sized sheets roasted seaweed (nori), cut into small squares

1. Line air fryer basket with parchment paper (unless it is nonstick) and preheat to 400°F. Place rice in a shallow bowl.
2. Place salmon in air fryer basket and air-fry 12 minutes.
3. Transfer salmon to the bowl on top of rice. Using a fork, flake and mix salmon into rice.
4. Add mayonnaise, soy sauce, salt, and pepper. Stir gently until combined.
5. Top with avocado, drizzle with sriracha, and garnish with seaweed pieces. Serve immediately.

Garlic Parmesan Chicken Tenders

It's hard to resist a crispy chicken tender, but these Garlic Parmesan Chicken Tenders steal the spotlight. This viral hit brings juicy chicken together with a rich, cheesy garlic sauce that's *sooo* ✨ cozy ✨ Easy to make at home and packed with flavor—there's no going back once you've tried them! Serve with ranch dressing or your fav dipping sauce.

SERVES 2

Chicken

1 cup buttermilk

2 teaspoons garlic powder, divided

1 teaspoon onion powder

1 teaspoon paprika

1 teaspoon cayenne pepper

1 teaspoon Italian seasoning

1 teaspoon salt

1 teaspoon ground white pepper

2 teaspoons ground black pepper, divided

1 pound boneless, skinless chicken breast, sliced into 2″-wide strips

½ cup all-purpose flour

¼ cup cornstarch

4 cups canola oil

Garlic Parmesan Sauce

4 tablespoons unsalted butter

4 cloves garlic, peeled and minced

1 teaspoon ground black pepper

¼ teaspoon crushed red pepper flakes

¾ cup heavy whipping cream

1 cup grated Parmesan cheese

3 tablespoons chopped fresh parsley

1. In a large bowl, stir together buttermilk, 1 teaspoon garlic powder, onion powder, paprika, cayenne pepper, Italian seasoning, salt, white pepper, and 1 teaspoon black pepper. Add chicken and stir to coat. Set aside to marinate at least 30 minutes.
2. In a shallow dish, mix flour, cornstarch, and remaining 1 teaspoon each garlic powder and black pepper until evenly combined.
3. In a large pot or fryer, heat oil to 350°F.
4. Remove chicken tenders from marinade and generously coat in flour mixture. Dip back in marinade, coat once more in flour mixture, and set aside on a wire rack.

5. Carefully fry 2 or 3 chicken tenders at a time 7–8 minutes until golden and crispy. Transfer cooked tenders to a wire rack or paper towel–lined plate to drain.
6. Make the Garlic Parmesan Sauce: In a medium saucepan over medium heat, melt butter. Add garlic, black pepper, and red pepper flakes and stir 1–2 minutes until fragrant. Slowly pour in cream, stirring gently, and bring to a simmer. Gradually stir in Parmesan until the sauce is thick and creamy, about 1 minute. Remove from heat and stir in parsley.
7. Using a silicone brush, coat chicken thoroughly with the sauce. Serve immediately.

For a spicy garlic Parmesan twist, add 2 tablespoons of Frank's RedHot sauce into the Garlic Parmesan Sauce 🔥

Million Dollar Spaghetti

Spaghetti got the ultimate upgrade thanks to the Internet! Combining rich, silky Alfredo with hearty, flavorful marinara and melted cheese, Million Dollar Spaghetti truly lives up to its fame. Comforting, indulgent, and *sooo* easy to make—every bite is worth a million bucks.

SERVES 8

¾ pound uncooked spaghetti
1 pound 85% lean ground beef
½ medium yellow onion, peeled and diced
1 medium green bell pepper, seeded and diced
1 teaspoon ground black pepper
2 teaspoons Italian seasoning, divided
2 teaspoons garlic powder, divided
2 teaspoons onion powder, divided
2 teaspoons salt, divided
1 (24-ounce) jar marinara sauce
4 tablespoons unsalted butter
3 teaspoons minced garlic
2 cups heavy whipping cream
1¾ cups grated Parmesan cheese, divided
Cracked black pepper
2 cups shredded mozzarella cheese
2 tablespoons chopped fresh parsley

1. Preheat oven to 350°F. Grease a 9″ × 13″ baking dish and set aside.
2. Cook spaghetti according to package instructions. Drain and set aside.
3. Make the meat sauce: In a large pot over high heat, cook beef with onion, bell pepper, ground black pepper, and 1 teaspoon each Italian seasoning, garlic powder, onion powder, and salt. Cook, stirring often, until beef is browned and veggies are translucent, 8–10 minutes.
4. Stir in marinara sauce and remaining 1 teaspoon each Italian seasoning, garlic powder, and onion powder. Reduce heat to medium-low and simmer 10 minutes.
5. Make the Alfredo sauce: In a large saucepan over medium heat, melt butter. Sauté garlic until fragrant, about 30 seconds. Add cream, 1 cup Parmesan cheese, cracked black pepper (about 10 cracks), and remaining 1 teaspoon salt. Stir continuously until smooth.

Continued

Continued

6. Add cooked spaghetti to the Alfredo sauce and toss until evenly coated. Spread spaghetti mixture in prepared baking dish.
7. Layer meat sauce over spaghetti. Top with mozzarella cheese and remaining ¾ cup Parmesan cheese.
8. Bake 15 minutes, then broil 5 minutes or until cheese is golden and bubbly.
9. Sprinkle with parsley, serve hot, and enjoy!

Chili Oil Noodles

Who doesn't love a warm, comfy bowl of noodles?! Easily made in just 10 minutes, this viral recipe packs a punch with bold, spicy flavor. But look out: These are super-spicy! They're perfect for anyone who craves the heat—are you up for the taste test?

SERVES 2

⅓ pound uncooked Taiwanese sliced noodles
1 tablespoon crushed red pepper flakes
1 teaspoon cayenne pepper
½ teaspoon granulated sugar
½ teaspoon salt
3 cloves garlic, peeled and minced
3 tablespoons chopped scallions, divided
3 tablespoons vegetable oil
1 medium shallot, peeled and minced
1 tablespoon soy sauce
1 tablespoon sesame oil
1 tablespoon light brown sugar
⅛ teaspoon MSG
1 tablespoon sesame seeds

1. Cook noodles according to package instructions. Drain and set aside.
2. In a large heatproof bowl, combine red pepper flakes, cayenne pepper, granulated sugar, salt, garlic, and 2 tablespoons scallions. Set aside.
3. In a small skillet over high heat, heat oil 30 seconds. Add shallot and fry 2–3 minutes until crispy and golden. Immediately pour hot oil and shallot over red pepper flake mixture—listen for that satisfying sizzle!
4. Add soy sauce, sesame oil, brown sugar, and MSG to chili oil mixture. Stir to combine.
5. Add cooked noodles to the chili oil sauce and toss until evenly coated.
6. Top with sesame seeds and remaining 1 tablespoon scallions. Serve immediately.

#ForYou Tips

Not so big on spice? You can adjust the spice level to your liking by reducing the crushed red pepper flakes to ½ tablespoon and/or the cayenne pepper to ½ teaspoon for a milder kick.

Smashburger Tacos

It's not a smashburger; it's not a taco—it's both. Combining the crispy crunch of a taco shell with the irresistible flavor of a smashburger, this juicy, delicious recipe doesn't mess around.

SERVES 6

½ cup mayonnaise
2 tablespoons sweet pickle relish
1 tablespoon mustard
½ teaspoon white wine vinegar
½ teaspoon onion powder
½ teaspoon garlic powder
½ teaspoon paprika
⅛ teaspoon ground white pepper
6 (6") flour tortillas
1 pound 80% lean ground beef
Salt
Ground black pepper
6 slices American cheese
¾ cup shredded lettuce
⅓ cup diced white onion
18 pickle chips

1. In a small bowl, combine mayonnaise, relish, mustard, vinegar, onion powder, garlic powder, paprika, and white pepper. Set aside.
2. Place tortillas on a flat surface. Form beef into six palm-sized balls (about 2½ ounces each). Flatten each beef ball evenly onto a tortilla, leaving about a ½" border around the edge. Season with salt and ground black pepper to taste.
3. Heat a large skillet over medium-high heat. Place each tortilla meat-side down and cook 2–4 minutes until beef is browned and crispy. Flip carefully. Immediately place 1 slice American cheese onto each taco. Cook another 2–3 minutes until cheese melts and tortilla is golden brown.
4. Remove from heat and top each taco with lettuce, onion, and pickle chips. Drizzle with mayonnaise mixture and season with salt and ground black pepper to taste. Fold each tortilla in half and serve immediately!

Flamin' Hot Cheetos Salad

Salads just got an irresistibly crunchy, fiery boost thanks to the viral Flamin' Hot Cheetos Salad. The airy crisp and addictive heat of Flamin' Hot Cheetos goes so perfectly with the refreshing cucumber, creamy avocado, and tangy burst of lime. Every bite is vibrant, flavorful, and totally worth the Internet hype!

SERVES 1

½ (8.5-ounce) bag Flamin' Hot Cheetos
1 medium cucumber, chopped
½ medium avocado, peeled, pitted, and chopped
2 tablespoons chopped fresh cilantro
Juice of ½ medium lime
1 tablespoon hot taco sauce
1 teaspoon Tajín seasoning

1. In a large bowl, combine Cheetos, cucumber, avocado, and cilantro. Stir gently to mix.
2. Squeeze lime juice over the salad.
3. Drizzle taco sauce on top and finish with a sprinkle of Tajín.
4. Serve immediately for maximum crunch and enjoy!

Baked Mac 'n' Cheese

Let's be honest—@tinekeyounger's baked mac 'n' cheese has had TikTok in a cheesy chokehold forever! Those corkscrew noodles? Total game-changer. And now you get to enjoy the Internet's *ultimate* mac 'n' cheese with a few extra twists for an easy, comfy meal whenever the craving hits. It's the best of both worlds, blending two perfect recipes into one dish that truly smacks 😋

SERVES 8

½ pound mozzarella cheese
½ pound sharp Cheddar cheese
½ pound smoked Gouda cheese
½ pound pepper jack cheese
2 tablespoons cornstarch
1 pound uncooked cavatappi pasta
3 tablespoons unsalted butter
3 tablespoons all-purpose flour
1 teaspoon onion powder
1 teaspoon smoked paprika
1 teaspoon ground mustard
1 teaspoon ground cayenne pepper
1 teaspoon salt
1 teaspoon ground black pepper
1 (12-ounce) can evaporated milk
1½ cups heavy cream
½ pound Velveeta, cubed

1. Shred mozzarella, Cheddar, Gouda, and pepper jack cheeses and place in a large bowl. Sprinkle with cornstarch and toss until evenly coated. Set aside.
2. Cook pasta according to package instructions, boiling 2 minutes less than the recommended time. Drain and set aside.
3. Preheat oven to 350°F. Grease a 9″ × 13″ baking dish.
4. In a large pot over medium-low heat, melt butter. Whisk in flour until combined, then whisk in onion powder, smoked paprika, mustard, cayenne pepper, salt, and black pepper.
5. Whisk in evaporated milk until smooth. Slowly add cream, whisking constantly. (If you pour it all at once, it could break the sauce or curdle.) Add Velveeta and whisk until melted and smooth.

Continued

Continued

6. Add half of the shredded cheese, a handful at a time. Whisk until smooth before adding more cheese. Add pasta and stir to coat.
7. Transfer half of the pasta and sauce mixture to prepared baking dish. Top with half of remaining cheese. Add remaining pasta and sauce mixture, then remaining cheese.
8. Bake 15–20 minutes until hot and bubbling, then broil 5 minutes.
9. Remove from oven and let rest about 5 minutes, then serve and enjoy!

Mix It Up

Not a big fan of Velveeta? You can swap it for another blendy cheese like mozzarella or Colby jack to give this dish a similar cheesy texture.

Bring It to a Party

Air Fryer Nachos

Nachos are a classic, but the air fryer takes them to a whole new level. This twist delivers the perfect combo of gooey cheese, crispy chips, and flavorful toppings.

SERVES 4

1 pound 85% lean ground beef
1 teaspoon ground cumin
1 teaspoon garlic powder
½ teaspoon paprika
1 (10-ounce) bag Doritos or tortilla chips
½ cup sliced black olives
1 medium tomato, diced
1 medium avocado, peeled, pitted, and diced
2 medium jalapeños, sliced
3 tablespoons chopped fresh cilantro, divided
1 cup shredded Cheddar cheese
1 cup shredded Monterey jack cheese
1 tablespoon sour cream

1. In a medium skillet over medium heat, add beef and season with cumin, garlic powder, and paprika. Cook, breaking up the meat with a wooden spoon, 4–5 minutes until browned and fully cooked. Drain any excess fat and set aside.
2. Preheat air fryer to 320°F.
3. Line air fryer basket with parchment paper. Create alternating layers of chips, beef, olives, tomato, avocado, jalapeños, 2 tablespoons cilantro, and both cheeses (saving a little cheese for the top layer) until the basket is about ¾ full. Air-fry 5–6 minutes until cheese is melted and bubbly.
4. Carefully lift nachos from the air fryer using parchment paper and transfer to a platter. Sprinkle with remaining cilantro and sour cream. Enjoy!

Crispy Parmesan Potatoes

These Crispy Parmesan Potatoes have exploded online, thanks to their drool-worthy taste and satisfying ASMR crunch. Golden brown and crunchy on the outside, and fluffy inside, they're *sooo* hard to resist. Pair them with ketchup, mayo, or your fav dipping sauce.

SERVES 8

4 large yellow potatoes, peeled and chopped

2 teaspoons salt, divided

4 tablespoons cornstarch

1 teaspoon ground black pepper

1 quart canola oil

¼ cup freshly grated Parmesan cheese

1 teaspoon chopped fresh chives

1. Fill a large saucepan with water and add potatoes and 1 teaspoon salt. Boil potatoes over high heat until they are easily pierced with a fork, 12–15 minutes. Drain and set aside to cool.
2. Mash potatoes with a fork until smooth, then push through a fine strainer into a medium bowl to remove lumps, ensuring the smoothest possible texture.
3. Stir in cornstarch, remaining 1 teaspoon salt, and pepper. Roll mixture into tablespoon-sized balls.
4. In a large pot or fryer, heat oil to 325°F. Fry potato balls 5–7 minutes in small batches until golden brown and crispy. Transfer cooked potato balls to a paper towel–lined plate to drain.
5. Place crispy potatoes in a serving bowl and top with Parmesan and chives. Serve immediately.

#ForYou Tips

For extra flavor, toss the hot potato balls in garlic butter or sprinkle them with more herbs before serving!

Butter Board

Step aside charcuterie—butter boards have officially taken over as the viral centerpiece of entertaining! This eye-catching trend is as stunning as it is delicious. Creamy butter is aesthetically swirled and topped with sweet, salty, and spicy garnishes.

SERVES 10

3 cups (6 sticks) unsalted butter, softened
1 large lemon
Flaky sea salt
2 tablespoons olive oil
6 cloves garlic, peeled and minced
2 tablespoons honey
½ teaspoon crushed red pepper flakes
Cracked black pepper
2 tablespoons chopped fresh chives
1 (4-ounce) package crostini slices

1. On a clean wooden board, spread softened butter into a ½"-thick layer across half of the board. Use a butter knife or small spatula to create decorative swirls, ensuring there are no visible gaps.
2. Evenly zest the lemon over the butter, making sure to cover all edges. Sprinkle generously with sea salt.
3. In a small saucepan over medium-low heat, heat oil 30 seconds. Sauté garlic about 2 minutes until lightly toasted and fragrant. Cool garlic oil 3–4 minutes, then drizzle evenly over the butter.
4. Drizzle honey over the butter in a thin stream. Sprinkle with red pepper flakes, black pepper, and chives.
5. Arrange crostini on remaining half of the board. Serve immediately and enjoy!

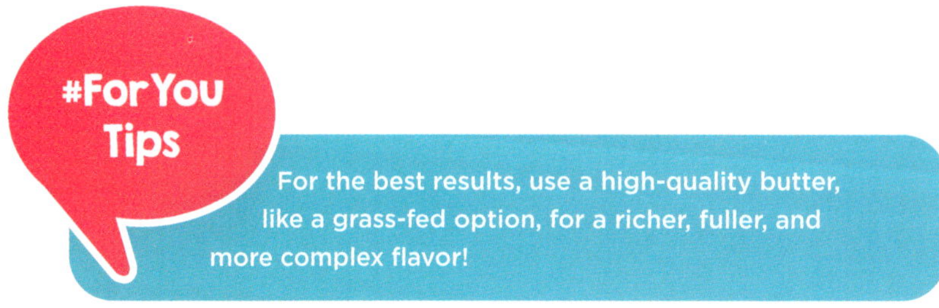

For the best results, use a high-quality butter, like a grass-fed option, for a richer, fuller, and more complex flavor!

Corn Ribs

Corn Ribs are a crispy, smoky, and superaddictive way to level up your veggie game. With their irresistible flavor and satisfying crunch, it's easy to see why this trending recipe has become the new must-have side at BBQs and potlucks.

SERVES: 4

4 large ears corn, shucked
2 teaspoons garlic powder
1 teaspoon onion powder
2½ teaspoons smoked paprika, divided
1 teaspoon ground cayenne pepper
3 teaspoons salt, divided
2 teaspoons ground black pepper
2 tablespoons olive oil
4 tablespoons unsalted butter, melted
2 cloves garlic, peeled and minced
½ cup mayonnaise
1 teaspoon paprika
1 teaspoon chipotle chili powder
1 tablespoon lime juice
¼ cup chopped fresh cilantro

1. Line air fryer basket with parchment paper (unless it is nonstick) and preheat to 375°F.
2. Carefully cut each ear of corn vertically into quarters, creating four "ribs" per ear. (Use a sharp knife and take it slow—it may require some force.)
3. In a small bowl, combine garlic powder, onion powder, 2 teaspoons smoked paprika, cayenne pepper, 2½ teaspoons salt, and black pepper.
4. Place corn ribs in a large bowl. Drizzle with oil and sprinkle seasoning blend evenly over corn. Toss until evenly coated.
5. Arrange corn ribs flat in air fryer basket (cook in batches if needed). Air-fry 12–15 minutes until crispy and slightly curled.
6. In a small bowl, combine butter and garlic. In another small bowl, mix mayonnaise, paprika, chipotle chili powder, lime juice, remaining smoked paprika, and remaining salt to create chipotle mayo sauce.
7. Drizzle garlic butter over corn ribs. Garnish with cilantro, and serve with chipotle mayo sauce. Enjoy!

Cowboy Caviar

Summer BBQs just wouldn't be the same without a big bowl of Cowboy Caviar 😋 This fresh, vibrant mix of beans, veggies, and zesty dressing is the perfect combo of crunchy, tangy, and refreshing vibes—and once you start scooping, you won't stop. Whether served as a dip or a side, this dish is gonna be the hit of the party!

SERVES 4–6

1 (15-ounce) can black-eyed peas, drained and rinsed

1 (15-ounce) can black beans, drained and rinsed

1 (15-ounce) can corn kernels, drained and rinsed

1 large tomato, diced

1 medium red onion, peeled and diced

1 medium red bell pepper, seeded and diced

1 medium green bell pepper, seeded and diced

1 medium avocado, peeled, pitted, and cubed

½ cup shredded lettuce

3 tablespoons diced jalapeño pepper

½ cup chopped fresh cilantro

½ cup Italian dressing

1 (12-ounce) bag restaurant-style tortilla chips

1. In a large bowl, combine black-eyed peas, black beans, corn, tomato, onion, bell peppers, avocado, lettuce, jalapeño, and cilantro.
2. Pour dressing over the mixture and toss until evenly coated.
3. Serve with tortilla chips and enjoy!

Pasta Chips

Move over, potatoes—there's a new chip in town! Thanks to the air fryer, the pasta in this recipe transforms into crispy, golden perfection, delivering a crunch that's pretty much impossible to resist. Whether you're serving them as a snack, an appetizer, or a girl dinner add-on, these cheesy, flavorful bites are worth the TikTok hype.

SERVES 2–4

1½ teaspoons salt, divided
½ pound uncooked bow tie pasta
2 tablespoons olive oil
1 teaspoon garlic powder
1 teaspoon paprika
1 teaspoon dried oregano
1 teaspoon ground black pepper
¼ teaspoon crushed red pepper flakes
½ cup shredded Parmesan cheese
½ cup marinara sauce

1. Adding 1 teaspoon salt to water in pot, cook pasta according to package instructions until al dente. Drain and transfer to a large bowl.
2. Line air fryer basket with parchment paper (unless it is nonstick) and preheat to 350°F.
3. Drizzle pasta with oil and season with garlic powder, paprika, oregano, black pepper, red pepper flakes, and remaining ½ teaspoon salt. Toss until evenly coated. Stir in Parmesan.
4. Place pasta in air fryer basket and air-fry 15 minutes, shaking the basket frequently to ensure even crisping.
5. Serve hot with a side of marinara sauce for dipping and enjoy!

#ForYou Tips

Using a smaller (3- or 2-quart) air fryer? Halve the recipe to avoid overcrowding—this ensures maximum crispiness!

Pull-Apart Holiday Cheese Bread

Nothing is quite as demure as a festive tree decorated with lights and your favorite ornaments. Except maybe a mini ✨ edible ✨ version! This tree-shaped holiday dish has been making its viral rounds on social media. The warm, pull-apart garlic and cheese bread balls served up with marinara sauce creates an aesthetic *and* delicious pizza-inspired appetizer.

SERVES 10–12

8 (1-ounce) mozzarella string cheese sticks
1 (13.8-ounce) can refrigerated pizza dough
2 tablespoons Italian seasoning
1 large egg, beaten
3 tablespoons unsalted butter, melted
3 cloves garlic, peeled and minced
1 teaspoon garlic powder
3 tablespoons chopped fresh parsley, divided
½ teaspoon salt
½ teaspoon ground black pepper
¼ cup grated Parmesan cheese
1 cup marinara sauce

1. Preheat oven to 375°F. Line a large baking sheet with parchment paper.
2. Cut each mozzarella stick into four equal pieces.
3. Roll out pizza dough into a rectangle on a cutting board, with a long side facing you. Cut the dough horizontally into four strips. Cut each strip vertically into eight squares. You will have thirty-two squares.
4. Place one cheese piece onto a dough square and sprinkle lightly with Italian seasoning. Carefully wrap the dough around the cheese, sealing it tightly to form a ball. Repeat with remaining cheese and dough pieces.
5. Arrange dough balls on prepared baking sheet in a Christmas tree shape, including a trunk. Start with a row of seven balls near the bottom of the sheet. Arrange six balls in a row above that. Continue adding rows, reducing the number of balls by one each time. Underneath the bottom row, arrange the last four balls in two rows of two balls each to form the trunk. Brush lightly and evenly with beaten egg.

Continued

Continued

6. Bake 16–18 minutes until golden brown.
7. While bread bakes, stir together butter, garlic, garlic powder, 2 tablespoons parsley, salt, and pepper in a small bowl.
8. Remove baking sheet from oven and immediately brush bread with garlic butter mixture. Sprinkle with Parmesan cheese and remaining 1 tablespoon parsley. Serve warm alongside marinara sauce for dipping.

Mix It Up

Don't wait around for the holiday season to try this out. You can arrange the cheese bread balls into any shape you want and dig in year-round!

Grilled Cheese Roll-Ups

Starting to feel hangry but don't have the time (or willpower) to spend forever in the kitchen? These famous Grilled Cheese Roll-Ups are perfect. Crispy on the outside, filled with gooey melted cheese, *and* supereasy to make, they're an irresistible snack that has taken over the Internet. Ready in just 10 minutes, they're guaranteed to be a hit!

SERVES 10

10 slices white bread
20 slices Colby jack cheese
2 tablespoons unsalted butter, melted
1 teaspoon garlic powder
1 cup marinara sauce, heated

1. Cut the crust off each slice of bread, then flatten slices gently using a rolling pin.
2. Place 2 slices cheese on each flattened bread slice, staggering them slightly to cover the bread fully.
3. Carefully roll up each bread slice, securing with toothpicks if needed.
4. In a small bowl, combine butter and garlic powder. Brush garlic butter over each roll-up.
5. Heat a large skillet over medium heat. Cook roll-ups in batches, 1–2 minutes per side until golden brown and cheese is melted.
6. Remove roll-ups from skillet, discard toothpicks, and serve immediately with marinara sauce for dipping. Enjoy!

Sweet Hawaiian Roll Sliders

These sweet Hawaiian rolls have been the hype all over TikTok! Loaded with ham and Swiss cheese, and topped with garlic sauce, this twist'll elevate your entertaining game to a 10.

SERVES 12

1 (12-count) package Hawaiian sweet rolls
¼ cup mayonnaise
½ pound sliced deli ham
6 slices Swiss cheese
1 tablespoon Dijon mustard
4 tablespoons unsalted butter, melted
2 cloves garlic, peeled and minced
½ teaspoon Worcestershire sauce
1 teaspoon onion powder
½ teaspoon dried oregano
½ teaspoon salt
2 tablespoons everything bagel seasoning

1. Preheat oven to 350°F and grease a 9″ × 13″ baking dish.
2. Keeping Hawaiian rolls connected, slice horizontally through the middle. Spread mayonnaise over the bottom half and place in prepared dish.
3. Layer ham slices evenly across rolls in dish, then top with Swiss cheese slices. Spread a thin layer of Dijon mustard across the cut side of the top half of the rolls, then place the top half over the bottom half.
4. In a small bowl, stir together butter, garlic, Worcestershire sauce, onion powder, oregano, and salt.
5. Brush butter mixture evenly over rolls. Bake 15–25 minutes until cheese is a little melty and bread is slightly golden brown.
6. Remove from oven and immediately sprinkle evenly with bagel seasoning. Serve warm.

#ForYou Tips

If the sliders don't separate easily after baking, use a small knife to cut through each slider before serving.

Queso Dip with Pretzel Bites

Thanks to Internet hacks, homemade pretzels have never been easier to make! Using just two ingredients, the dough in this recipe became an instant sensation—and creates the perfect match for the warm, spicy queso dip. Serve at your next hangout and watch your friends swarm for a taste.

SERVES 4–6

1¾ cups self-rising flour
1¼ cups plain low-fat Greek yogurt
3 cups water
¼ cup baking soda
1 large egg, beaten
Coarse sea salt
½ cup shredded sharp Cheddar cheese
½ cup shredded mozzarella cheese
½ cup shredded pepper jack cheese
4 ounces cream cheese
⅔ cup queso cheese dip
¼ cup beer or dry white wine
1 teaspoon garlic powder
2 teaspoons chipotle chili powder

1. Preheat oven to 450°F.
2. In a medium bowl, combine flour and yogurt, kneading until the dough forms a ball. Turn onto a lightly floured surface and knead briefly until smooth. Divide into ten equal-sized balls (about 2″ each).
3. In a large pot over high heat, bring water and baking soda to a rolling boil. Drop pretzel balls into the water and boil 30 seconds. Remove balls with a slotted spoon and arrange them around the edges of a greased 10″ oven-safe skillet.
4. Brush balls with beaten egg and sprinkle with sea salt.
5. In a medium bowl, mix together Cheddar, mozzarella, pepper jack, cream cheese, queso dip, beer, garlic powder, and chipotle chili powder until fully combined. Pour cheese mixture into the center of prepared skillet.
6. Bake 20 minutes then broil on high 5 minutes or until golden and bubbly. Remove from oven and let cool 10 minutes before serving.

Baked Brie Puff Pastry

This festive dish has been making the rounds on social media, becoming an absolute showstopper at every gathering. Topped with fresh thyme, sweet honey, and tangy cranberry sauce, a whole round of soft Brie cheese is wrapped in golden, flaky puff pastry. *Sooo* cozy! Celebrate holidays, parties, and even just regular weekdays with the most decadent appetizer there is.

SERVES 12

1 (10" × 15") sheet puff pastry, thawed
1 (8-ounce) wheel Brie cheese
2 tablespoons cranberry sauce
1 teaspoon fresh thyme leaves
3 tablespoons finely chopped almonds
1 tablespoon honey
1 large egg, beaten
1 medium apple, cored and thinly sliced
Toasted wheat crackers
Nut Thins crackers

1. Preheat oven to 400°F. Line a large baking sheet with parchment paper.
2. Place puff pastry on prepared baking sheet and set Brie in the center. With a sharp knife, lightly score the top of the Brie to allow steam to escape. Spread cranberry sauce evenly on top, then sprinkle with thyme and almonds. Drizzle with honey.
3. Gently fold puff pastry over Brie, creating folds as you go. Brush edges with egg to secure each fold, ensuring cheese is fully enclosed.
4. Brush entire pastry with egg, then lightly score the top with a paring knife for decoration.
5. Bake 30–35 minutes until pastry is golden and puffed.
6. Allow to cool at least 5 minutes before serving. Serve warm with apple slices and crackers. Enjoy!

Nashville Hot Fried Mozzarella Slabs

Everything tastes better with the chili heat of Nashville-style hot oil sauce 🔥 Mozzarella has now entered the chat, using this sauce, once popular with chicken, for a seriously delicious combo of cheesy and spicy goodness. These Nashville Hot Fried Mozzarella Slabs have gone viral, and it's become an Internet challenge to see who can get the best cheese pull. This recipe is perfect for a party platter alongside ranch for dipping—and those Texas hold 'em vibes. Yeehaw!

SERVES 8

1½ cups plain bread crumbs
1 teaspoon onion powder
2 teaspoons garlic powder, divided
1 teaspoon smoked paprika
2 teaspoons cayenne pepper, divided
2 teaspoons salt, divided
1½ teaspoons ground black pepper, divided
1 cup all-purpose flour
3 large eggs, beaten
1 (8-ounce) block mozzarella cheese
1 tablespoon light brown sugar
1 teaspoon chili powder
½ teaspoon paprika
4 cups canola oil

1. Line a large baking sheet with parchment paper.
2. In a shallow bowl, combine bread crumbs, onion powder, 1 teaspoon garlic powder, smoked paprika, 1 teaspoon cayenne pepper, 1 teaspoon salt, and 1 teaspoon black pepper. Place flour in another shallow bowl and eggs in a third shallow bowl.
3. Cut mozzarella block into slabs about 1" thick. Dip a mozzarella slab in flour, then eggs, and then bread crumb mixture. Dip the slab in eggs again and finally in bread crumb mixture again. Press firmly to fully coat the cheese. Place coated slab onto prepared baking sheet. Repeat with remaining slabs. Freeze 30 minutes to 1 hour.
4. In a medium heatproof bowl, combine sugar, chili powder, paprika, and remaining 1 teaspoon garlic powder, 1 teaspoon cayenne pepper, 1 teaspoon salt, and ½ teaspoon black pepper. Set aside.

Continued

Continued

5. Heat oil in a large, deep pot over medium-high heat until it reaches 350°F. Fry mozzarella slabs in batches of 1–3 at a time to avoid crowding. Fry each slab about 2 minutes or until golden brown. Transfer to a wire rack to drain.
6. Carefully remove ½ cup of hot frying oil and immediately pour it into spice mixture bowl. Stir until fully combined.
7. Dip or brush each mozzarella slab with hot oil sauce, ensuring each is evenly coated on all sides.
8. Serve immediately and enjoy!

International Delights

Dubai Chocolate Bar

Pistachios got a serious glow-up once Dubai put its magic touch on them, turning out the most stunning, delicious chocolate bars that everyone suddenly wanted in on. These bars don't just look good—they bring all the ASMR vibes 🥰 You can find kataifi (a fine, vermicelli-like pastry) in Middle Eastern grocery stories, online, or in some chain supermarkets in the international section.

SERVES 1–2

1 tablespoon canola oil

2 cups chopped kataifi

1 cup pistachio paste

¼ cup white chocolate chips, melted

8 ounces semisweet baking chocolate, chopped

1. In a large skillet over medium heat, heat oil 30 seconds. Add kataifi and cook, stirring, 2–3 minutes until golden. Transfer to a paper towel–lined plate and set aside to cool 5 minutes.
2. Transfer kataifi to a medium bowl and add pistachio paste. Stir gently until combined. This is your filling.
3. In a deep, silicone chocolate bar mold, drizzle melted white chocolate in fun abstract patterns. Set aside.
4. Place semisweet chocolate in the top of a double boiler or a heatproof bowl set over a pan of simmering water. Stir constantly until melted, being careful not to let the temperature exceed 90°F so chocolate does not lose its temper. Pour some of the melted chocolate into the mold, painting it up the sides using a spoon or a silicone brush. Refrigerate 15–20 minutes until the layer has completely set.
5. Remove chocolate mold from the refrigerator and pipe or spoon pistachio mixture over the chocolate shell.
6. Remelt remaining chocolate if necessary. Cover the pistachio layer with a layer of chocolate. Refrigerate 15–20 minutes until hardened.
7. Pop the chocolate out of the mold and enjoy!

Tanghulu

When the Internet discovered Tanghulu, it was love at first crunch. This glossy, candied fruit treat became an instant hit for its elegant simplicity and satisfying crack. TikTok couldn't get enough of the mesmerizing candy shells, and neither will you. This version is guaranteed to turn heads and deliver the ultimate ASMR-worthy bite.

SERVES 4

12 pieces of fruit (small strawberries, grapes, or mandarin orange slices)
2 cups granulated sugar
1 cup water

1. Skewer 3 pieces of fruit onto a wooden skewer. Repeat with three more skewers and remaining fruit. Set aside.
2. Fill a large bowl with ice cubes and water to make an ice water bath.
3. In a medium saucepan, combine sugar and 1 cup water. Heat over medium-high heat without stirring until mixture reaches exactly 300°F. Use a candy thermometer for accuracy.
4. Remove pan from heat. Quickly dip and rotate each fruit skewer in the syrup until fully coated.
5. Immediately submerge the coated skewers into the ice water bath 10–15 seconds to set the candy shell. Place skewers on a parchment-lined tray or cooling rack to finish hardening.
6. Serve immediately.

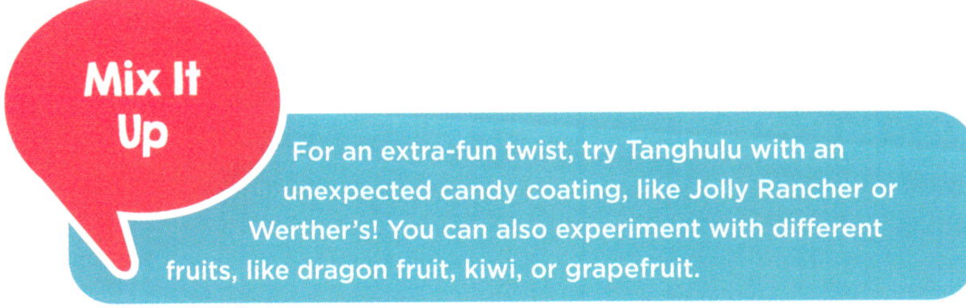

Brazilian Lemonade

Nothing beats that refreshing taste of a cold lemonade—except Brazilian Lemonade. In Brazil, lemons take a back seat to limes. Yep, limes! But Brazilian lemonade is anything but bitter; sweetened condensed milk is blended in for a creamy touch that lightens up the citrus. You'll be coming back for more of this quencher.

SERVES 2

3 medium limes, peeled, plus 2 slices for garnish
1 cup water
1 cup ice
1 (14-ounce) can sweetened condensed milk

1. Cut limes into wedges and place in a blender. Add water and blend 1 minute at high speed until smooth. Strain mixture to remove pulp.
2. Pour strained liquid back into the blender. Add ice and condensed milk, then blend 1 minute at high speed until smooth and creamy.
3. Serve immediately, garnishing with lime slices, and enjoy!

French Hot Chocolate

France has got hot chocolate down to an art. This thick, velvety, and indulgent French Hot Chocolate has taken over the Internet for its almost dessert-like texture. Rich melted chocolate blends with warm milk to create a café-worthy drink that feels as boujee as sipping ganache. Top it off with a dollop of whipped cream, and you've got the ultimate hot chocolate experience.

SERVES 2

2 cups whole milk
¼ cup brewed coffee
¾ cup sweetened condensed milk
6 ounces semisweet baking chocolate, chopped
4 teaspoons vanilla extract, divided
1 teaspoon ground cinnamon, plus more for garnish
⅛ teaspoon ground nutmeg, plus more for garnish
⅛ teaspoon salt
1 cup heavy whipping cream
1 teaspoon confectioners' sugar

1. In a medium saucepan over low heat, combine whole milk, coffee, condensed milk, chocolate, 2 teaspoons vanilla, 1 teaspoon cinnamon, ⅛ teaspoon nutmeg, and salt. Stir frequently and let mixture simmer 30 minutes or until thick and creamy.
2. In a small bowl, combine cream, remaining vanilla, and sugar. Using an electric mixer set to medium-high speed or a whisk, beat about 3 minutes until soft peaks form.
3. Pour hot chocolate into two mugs and top generously with whipped cream.
4. Garnish with a sprinkle of cinnamon and nutmeg, then serve immediately.

Mochi Donuts

Mochi Donuts are the perfect blend of beauty and taste. The flowery shape, bright colors, and fun designs have made them a viral sensation. And the sweet, chewy texture keeps everyone coming back for more. These donuts aren't just a treat—they're an ✨ experience ✨

MAKES 8 DONUTS

Donuts

1½ cups whole milk
½ cup granulated sugar
4 tablespoons unsalted butter
1 teaspoon salt
4 cups glutinous rice flour
¼ cup tapioca starch
2 large eggs
4 teaspoons baking powder
4 cups canola oil

Matcha Glaze

1½ cups confectioners' sugar
3 tablespoons whole milk
3 teaspoons matcha powder
4 ounces white chocolate, melted

Strawberry Glaze

1½ cups confectioners' sugar
¼ cup whole milk
4½ teaspoons powdered freeze-dried strawberries
1 (4-ounce) bar semisweet baking chocolate, melted

Donuts

1. In a large saucepan over medium-high heat, combine milk, granulated sugar, butter, and salt. Bring to a boil. Add flour and tapioca starch all at once. Immediately reduce heat to low and stir until a firm, sticky dough forms, about 2 minutes. (It will start clumpy but smooth out as you stir.)
2. Transfer dough to a stand mixer fitted with a dough hook attachment. Knead on medium speed about 2 minutes to release steam. Scrape down sides, then add 1 egg. Knead again on medium until incorporated, about 1 minute. Add remaining egg and knead another minute until smooth.

Continued

Continued

3. Add baking powder and knead 1 additional minute until fully combined. The dough will be sticky—that's the signature chewy texture!
4. Cut out eight squares of parchment (about 5″ × 5″ each). Form dough into sixty-four small balls, about ½ tablespoon each. Place eight balls in a circle onto each parchment square. Repeat to create eight donuts.
5. Heat oil in a large, deep pot over medium-high heat until it reaches 350°F. Carefully lower each donut (with parchment still attached) into hot oil. Fry until donuts float and become golden, about 2–3 minutes. Once the donuts rise, remove parchment paper. Transfer donuts to a wire rack lined with paper towels to drain.

Matcha Glaze

In a shallow bowl, whisk confectioners' sugar, milk, and matcha powder until smooth. Dip four donuts into glaze, gently shaking off excess. Let dry slightly. Drizzle white chocolate lightly over one side of glazed donuts.

Strawberry Glaze

In another shallow bowl, whisk confectioners' sugar, milk, and strawberry powder. Dip remaining four donuts into glaze, gently shaking off excess. Let dry slightly. Drizzle semisweet chocolate lightly over one side of glazed donuts.

Turkish Pasta

Turkish Pasta is blowing up all over TikTok thanks to an irresistible combo of delicious Mediterranean flavors and easy steps. Every ingredient perfectly complements the next—from the caramelized beef to the creamy garlic yogurt sauce to the warm paprika butter drizzle. Inspired by the Internet fav, this recipe is hearty, comforting, and so simple you'll wanna make it again and again.

SERVES 4–6

¾ pound uncooked bow tie pasta
1 pound 85% lean ground beef
¼ teaspoon curry powder
1 teaspoon ground black pepper
2 teaspoons onion powder
1 teaspoon paprika
1½ teaspoons salt, divided
½ medium yellow onion, peeled and diced
1 cup plain whole-milk Greek yogurt
3 cloves garlic, peeled and minced
4 tablespoons unsalted butter
3 teaspoons sweet paprika
½ cup halved cherry tomatoes
¼ cup chopped fresh parsley

1. Cook pasta according to package instructions until al dente. Drain and set aside.
2. In a large skillet over medium-high heat, add beef, curry powder, pepper, onion powder, paprika, and 1 teaspoon salt. Sauté 5 minutes, breaking up the meat with a wooden spoon.
3. Add onion and cook 8–10 minutes, stirring often, until beef is browned and onion is caramelized.
4. In a medium bowl, combine yogurt, garlic, and remaining ½ teaspoon salt. Set aside.
5. In a small saucepan over medium heat, melt butter. Stir in sweet paprika and cook 1–2 minutes until combined.
6. Divide pasta among individual bowls. Top each serving with garlic yogurt sauce and crispy beef. Drizzle with paprika butter sauce and top with tomatoes and parsley. Stir and enjoy!

Korean Corn Dogs

Nothing captures the vibe of fair food quite like a Korean Corn Dog. It's the best of the best—crispy, cheesy, and downright irresistible. Whether you're sticking to the traditional ingredients here or going full-on viral with creative coatings like ramen, corn flakes, or sugar, these corn dogs are bound to steal the show.

SERVES 4

4 hot dogs, cut in half crosswise

4 (1-ounce) mozzarella string cheese sticks, cut in half crosswise

1½ cups all-purpose flour

2 tablespoons plus 1 teaspoon granulated sugar, divided

2 teaspoons baking powder

¼ teaspoon salt

1 large egg

½ cup whole milk

1 cup diced frozen French fries

1 cup plain bread crumbs

4 cups canola oil

1. Skewer a hot dog half and a mozzarella stick half onto a wooden skewer, then place on a baking sheet. Repeat with remaining hot dogs and cheese sticks. Refrigerate skewers while you prepare the batter and coating.
2. In a medium bowl, whisk together flour, 2 tablespoons sugar, baking powder, and salt. Add egg and milk, stirring until the batter is thick and smooth. Transfer to a tall glass or jar for easy dipping, then refrigerate 15–20 minutes.
3. Spread diced French fries in a shallow dish and bread crumbs in another shallow dish.
4. Heat oil in a large, deep pot over medium-high heat until it reaches 350°F.
5. Remove skewers and batter from the refrigerator. Dip each skewer into the chilled batter, rotating to coat evenly. Roll immediately in diced French fries, pressing gently to help them stick. Then dip in bread crumbs, ensuring full coverage.
6. Fry in batches 3–4 minutes, turning occasionally, until golden brown and crispy. Use tongs to transfer fried corn dogs to a wire rack to drain. Sprinkle lightly with remaining 1 teaspoon sugar and enjoy.

Birria Tacos

Popular in Mexico for decades, Birria Tacos are *finally* getting their viral moment 🥰 These crispy tacos are packed with juicy, melt-in-your-mouth beef, and are perfectly spiced and bursting with flavor. Deliciously messy, they'll have your mouth watering at first sight. Get ready for a meal that feels like pure fantasy—just make sure you've got a lot of napkins ready!

SERVES 4–8

2 whole cloves
½ cinnamon stick
2 bay leaves
4 guajillo chilies
3 ancho chilies
2 New Mexico red chilies
2 cups beef broth
4–5 pounds chuck roast
3 teaspoons salt, divided
2 teaspoons ground black pepper, divided
2 tablespoons vegetable oil
1 large white onion, peeled and chopped
1 head garlic, cloves separated and peeled
1 teaspoon ground sage
1 tablespoon ground cumin
2 teaspoons dried oregano
2 tablespoons chicken bouillon powder
3 sprigs fresh mint
2 tablespoons apple cider vinegar
8–10 (4") corn tortillas
12 ounces (about 2 cups) Oaxaca cheese, shredded
½ medium yellow onion, peeled and diced
¼ cup chopped fresh cilantro
2 medium limes, cut into wedges

1. Make a spice bundle: Wrap cloves, cinnamon stick, and bay leaves in cheesecloth or a coffee filter and tie with a string. Set aside.
2. Remove stems and seeds from dried chilies and place in a medium saucepan. Add broth and bring to a boil over medium-high heat. Reduce heat to medium-low and simmer 10–15 minutes until soft.
3. While chilies simmer, season chuck roast on all sides with 2 teaspoons salt and 1 teaspoon black pepper. In a large skillet over medium-high heat, heat oil 30 seconds. Add beef and sear until browned on all sides, about 2 minutes per side. Transfer beef to a slow cooker.

4. In the same skillet, sauté white onion and garlic 3–4 minutes over medium heat until slightly softened. Pour simmered chilies and broth into skillet. Add sage, cumin, oregano, bouillon powder, and remaining 1 teaspoon each salt and black pepper. Cook 5–7 minutes, then transfer to a blender and blend 2–3 minutes at medium speed until smooth.
5. Pour blended sauce over beef in the slow cooker, ensuring it's fully coated. Add spice bundle. Cook on low 6–8 hours or on high 4–5 hours until beef is fall-apart tender.
6. Stir in mint sprigs and apple cider vinegar, cover, and cook 15 minutes. Remove and discard spice bundle and mint sprigs. Shred beef with two forks. Skim excess oil from the sauce (consommé) and reserve for dipping.
7. Scoop out a spoonful of consommé and pour it into a medium skillet over medium-high heat. Place a tortilla in skillet and turn to coat both sides. Sprinkle cheese on one side of tortilla, then layer shredded beef on top. Fold tortilla in half and cook 4–5 minutes per side until crispy. Repeat for remaining tacos.
8. Garnish tacos with yellow onion and cilantro. Squeeze a lime wedge over each taco. Serve alongside a small bowl of consommé for dipping.

No Crock-Pot? Cook this recipe in a Dutch oven at 220°F 4–5 hours until the beef is *suuuper* tender. If you have any leftovers, you can add them into other foods such as mac 'n' cheese, burrito bowls, grilled cheese sandwiches, etc.

Ube Mini Cheesecakes

Ube's bright purple hue is instantly recognizable, but its subtly sweet, nutty flavor is what *really* makes it unforgettable. These Ube Mini Cheesecakes have taken over social media thanks to the stunning color and indulgent texture—plus they're mini-sized for the perfect bite. With a buttery graham cracker base and a luscious ube-infused filling, these favs are the ultimate blend of Filipino flavors and OG cheesecake decadence.

SERVES 12

Crust

1 cup graham cracker crumbs (or 8 whole graham crackers, crushed)

¼ cup unsalted butter, melted

½ teaspoon salt

Cheesecake Filling

1 cup heavy whipping cream

1 (8-ounce) package cream cheese, softened

12 ounces ube jam

1 cup confectioners' sugar

2 teaspoons lemon juice

½ teaspoon ube extract

½ teaspoon salt

Ganache Topping

2½ tablespoons heavy whipping cream

2 (4-ounce) bars white baking chocolate, chopped

2 drops ube extract

¼ cup sweetened shredded coconut

Crust

1. Line a twelve-cup muffin tin with paper liners.
2. Place graham crumbs in a food processor. Add butter and salt and pulse until mixture resembles wet sand. Press mixture firmly into the bottoms of the muffin tin cups, filling each about ¼ full.

Cheesecake Filling

1. In a large bowl, add cream. Using an electric mixer set to medium-high speed or a whisk, beat about 4 minutes until stiff peaks form. Set aside.

Continued

Continued

2. In a separate large bowl, add cream cheese and beat on medium-high speed about 4 minutes until smooth. Add ube jam, sugar, lemon juice, ube extract, and salt. Mix until fully combined.
3. Gently fold in whipped cream until mixture is smooth and airy. Spoon Cheesecake Filling into the muffin cups, smoothing the tops. Refrigerate at least 6 hours, preferably overnight, to set.

Ganache Topping

1. In a medium microwave-safe bowl, add cream and microwave on high 20 seconds or until warm but not boiling. Add chocolate and ube extract, stirring until smooth. If needed, microwave in 2-second intervals, stirring after each interval to avoid seizing.
2. Remove cheesecakes from muffin tin and drizzle each with Ganache Topping.
3. Top with coconut, serve, and enjoy!

You can also pop these in the freezer for a few hours before serving if you want a firmer consistency.

Hong Kong French Toast

Hong Kong has redefined breakfast, and this indulgent creation is proof they're way ahead of the curve. Layers of peanut butter, a crispy cornflake crust, and a drizzle of sweet condensed milk? Pure breakfast delight. It's rich, it's crunchy, and it's downright irresistible. One bite, and you'll wonder why anyone ever settled for plain toast.

SERVES 1

3 slices white bread
¼ cup smooth peanut butter
2 large eggs
2 teaspoons whole milk
1 teaspoon vanilla extract
1 cup crushed cornflakes
½ cup vegetable oil
2 tablespoons sweetened condensed milk

1. Trim the crusts off the bread, then spread a generous layer of peanut butter between the slices to create a three-layer sandwich.
2. In a shallow dish, whisk together eggs, milk, and vanilla until smooth. Place crushed cornflakes in another shallow dish.
3. Dip sandwich into egg mixture, ensuring it's fully coated, then press it into cornflakes to cover every side.
4. Heat oil in a large, deep skillet over medium heat until it reaches 300°F.
5. Fry sandwich 2–5 minutes, flipping halfway through, until golden and crispy.
6. Drizzle with condensed milk for the ultimate finish. Serve immediately and enjoy!

Hwachae

Noticing your FYP is full of influencers sipping on cool, refreshing Hwachae? This modern-day fruit salad from Korea has taken over social media for a reason—it's colorful, customizable, and totally fun. A mix of fresh fruit, jellies, and popping boba blended with your favorite drink, any concoction goes!

SERVES 3

2 cups cubed watermelon
½ cup blueberries
½ cup sliced strawberries
4 fruit jelly cups, diced
½ cup popping boba
1 cup ice
1 cup Starbucks Pink Drink
1 cup Sprite soda

1. In a large bowl, combine watermelon, blueberries, strawberries, fruit jelly, and popping boba.
2. Add ice, Pink Drink, and Sprite. Mix gently, serve in cups or bowls, and enjoy this refreshing treat!

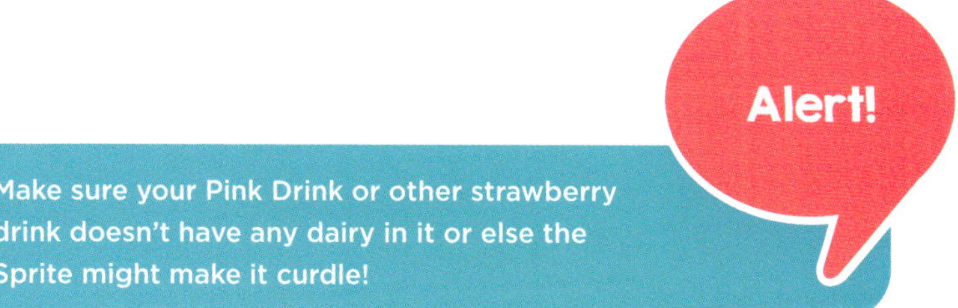

Korean Marshmallow Ice Cream Bar

Imagine a creamy, frozen center wrapped in a warm roasted-marshmallow shell, and when you bite into it, you get that perfect blend of chewy, fluffy, and melt-in-your-mouth goodness 🤤 It's real! But TBH, the best part is toasting that marshmallow layer with a blowtorch.

SERVES 1

1 empty (8-ounce) box shelf-stable milk
8–10 marshmallows
1 chocolate-covered ice cream bar on a stick

1. Cut the top off the milk box, lightly grease the inside, and set aside.
2. In a large bowl, microwave marshmallows on high in 2 (30-second) intervals until smooth and gooey. Scoop marshmallow fluff into prepared milk box, filling it about ⅔ full.
3. Insert ice cream bar into marshmallow mixture, ensuring the coating completely covers the bar up to the stick. Trim the sides of the ice cream bar to fit if needed. Freeze overnight until fully set.
4. Carefully cut and peel away the milk box to release the ice cream bar.
5. Using a blowtorch, gently toast the marshmallow coating until golden and slightly crisp.

Alert!

A blowtorch is used for this recipe. Follow any safety instructions on the packaging/equipment and make sure any kids in the kitchen are accompanied by someone 18 or older.

Japanese Fried Whipped Cream Sandwiches

Sure, Japanese whipped cream sandwiches are amazing, but *fried* whipped cream sandwiches?! The light, refreshing cream paired with a crispy, golden crunch is next-level perfection. Add in your favorite fruits, matcha, or even chocolate for a TikTok-worthy twist. These are the ultimate upgrade from your ordinary snack. Trust me—you'll be craving 'em for weeks.

SERVES 2

1½ cups cold heavy cream
½ cup confectioners' sugar
1 teaspoon vanilla extract
4 cups canola oil
4 thick slices white bread
½ cup sliced strawberries
2 tablespoons chocolate syrup

1. In a large bowl, combine cream, sugar, and vanilla. Using an electric mixer set to medium-high speed or a whisk, beat about 5 minutes until stiff peaks form. Refrigerate until ready to use.
2. Heat oil in a large, deep skillet over medium heat until it reaches 350°F. Fry bread slices 2–3 minutes per side until golden and crisp,. Let cool slightly.
3. Cut each fried bread slice into triangles, then carefully cut through the edge of each triangle to create a pocket.
4. Fill bread pockets with whipped cream and top with strawberries. Drizzle with chocolate syrup and serve.

Soup Dumplings

Sometimes you're craving dumplings, but making them from scratch or ordering out isn't superrealistic. Thankfully, this TikTok-inspired hack makes delicious Soup Dumplings possible in just *5 minutes*. With a savory pork and ginger filling and a perfectly balanced umami sauce, it's easy to see why everyone's obsessed!

SERVES 2–3

1 (6-ounce) package frozen pork and ginger soup dumplings
½ cup chicken broth
1 tablespoon soy sauce
2 scallions, thinly sliced
1 teaspoon chili crisp, plus extra for topping.
1 teaspoon sesame oil
Toasted sesame seeds

1. Place dumplings in a medium skillet with a small amount of water (about ¼ cup). Cover and steam over medium heat about 5 minutes, until dumplings are soft and heated through.
2. While dumplings steam, mix chicken broth, soy sauce, scallions, 1 teaspoon chili crisp, and oil in a small bowl. Microwave on high 2–3 minutes until hot.
3. Transfer steamed dumplings to a serving plate and pour broth mixture evenly over the top.
4. Top each dumpling with a small spoonful of chili crisp and sprinkle sesame seeds on top. Serve immediately and enjoy!

CHAPTER 6

Sweet Treats

Frozen Strawberry Yogurt Bites

If there's one thing TikTok can't resist, it's the satisfying crunch of solidified chocolate breaking. It's the kind of ASMR that makes viral recipes so addictive. These Frozen Strawberry Yogurt Bites strike the perfect balance of indulging and refreshing, making them an ideal treat for any time of day. Whether you're whipping them up as a breakfast hack, quick snack, or late-night craving, these bites are totally worth the hype!

SERVES 4–6

1 cup plain whole-milk Greek yogurt
1 cup chopped strawberries
3 (4-ounce) bars semisweet baking chocolate, chopped

1. Line a large baking sheet with parchment paper.
2. In a medium bowl, mix together yogurt and strawberries.
3. Scoop mixture into small clusters (about ¼ cup each) and place them on prepared baking sheet. Freeze overnight until firm.
4. Place chocolate in the top of a double boiler or a heatproof bowl set over a pan of simmering water. Stir constantly until melted, being careful not to let the temperature exceed 90°F.
5. Dip each frozen yogurt cluster in melted chocolate and turn to coat completely. Return clusters to the parchment-lined baking sheet.
6. Freeze 1 hour to set.
7. Serve straight from the freezer and enjoy!

Biscoff Nutella Brownies

If brownies are your go-to treat, then this viral mash-up is a *must*. It's not just indulgent Nutella—it's Nutella and Biscoff together, creating the ultimate layered dessert. The trick? Freezing the spreads ensures perfect layers inside the brownies, making every bite rich, gooey, and utterly irresistible. Warm 'em up, pair 'em with a glass of milk, and you'll have a hard time not going back for seconds (and thirds!).

SERVES 16

½ cup Nutella hazelnut spread

½ cup Biscoff creamy cookie butter spread

¾ cup (1½ sticks) unsalted butter

3 (4-ounce) bars semisweet baking chocolate, chopped and divided

1½ cups granulated sugar

3 large eggs

½ cup cocoa powder

2 teaspoons vanilla extract

1 teaspoon salt

1 cup all-purpose flour

1. Line two large baking sheets with parchment paper.
2. Scoop Nutella onto one prepared baking sheet. Spread it into a thin 8″ × 8″ square layer. Scoop Biscoff onto the other prepared baking sheet and spread it into a thin 8″ × 8″ square layer. Freeze overnight or until firm.
3. Preheat oven to 325°F. Grease an 8″ × 8″ baking pan and line it with parchment paper.
4. In a medium microwave-safe bowl, melt butter with 6 ounces chocolate in 20-second intervals, stirring between each until smooth. Let cool slightly.
5. In a medium bowl, whisk sugar and eggs together 30 seconds. Add cocoa and whisk until fully combined. Gradually mix cooled chocolate mixture into egg and sugar mixture. Stir in vanilla and salt.
6. Gently fold flour into chocolate mixture until just combined. Stir in remaining 6 ounces chopped chocolate, being careful not to overmix.
7. Spread half of the brownie batter onto prepared pan.

Continued

Continued

8. Carefully place the frozen Nutella layer on top, then cover with remaining brownie batter. Top with the frozen Biscoff layer.
9. Use a butter knife to create gentle swirls for a marbled effect. Bake 30 minutes or until a toothpick inserted in the center comes out with a few moist crumbs.
10. Allow brownies to cool completely before cutting into squares. Serve and enjoy the gooey, layered perfection!

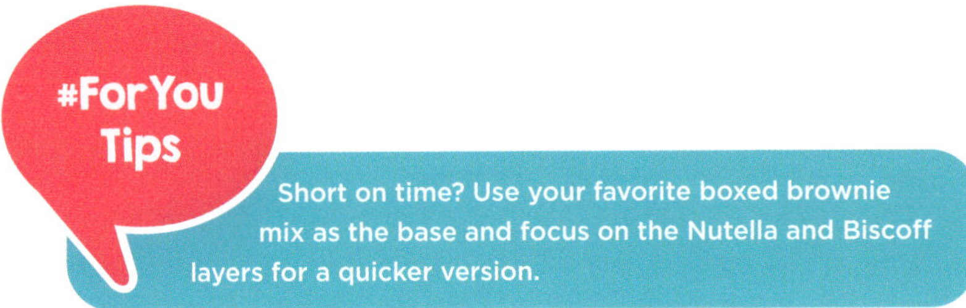

Baked Oats

One of the top trends of the Internet is baked oats, probably because they're *sooo* customizable. From sweet breakfast treats to decadent desserts, there are variations on this recipe for every craving, every season, and every time of day! Use this as a base for your own spin-offs.

SERVES 1

½ medium ripe banana, peeled
1 large egg
½ cup rolled oats
1 teaspoon vanilla extract
¼ cup whole milk
½ teaspoon baking powder
½ teaspoon salt
⅔ cup semisweet chocolate chips

1. Preheat oven to 350°F. Spray a small baking dish with nonstick cooking spray.
2. In a blender, combine banana, egg, oats, vanilla, milk, baking powder, and salt. Blend 1 minute at high speed until smooth.
3. Pour batter into prepared baking dish. Sprinkle chocolate chips on top and gently fold them into the batter.
4. Bake 20–25 minutes until golden and set. Serve warm and enjoy immediately!

Air Fryer S'mores Dip

When sweet cravings hit, the Internet's favorite kitchen gadget—the air fryer—always delivers! This viral Air Fryer S'mores Dip is no exception, bringing all the deliciousness of the classic campfire treat but with less mess and more convenience. It's one dessert you'll definitely wanna hit "Save" on!

SERVES 2

16–20 jumbo marshmallows
2 (4-ounce) bars semisweet baking chocolate
10 graham crackers, broken into quarters

1. Preheat air fryer to 375°F. Line air fryer basket with foil or parchment paper.
2. Arrange marshmallows tightly together in rows, covering the bottom of the air fryer in one layer.
3. Air-fry about 5 minutes until marshmallows are fluffy and golden brown.
4. Break chocolate bars into pieces and place between marshmallows. Air-fry another 2 minutes or until chocolate is melted.
5. Serve immediately with graham crackers for dipping.

Mix It Up

Swap out the chocolate bars for Reese's peanut butter cups to level up the flavor! You can also use white chocolate, or cookies and cream chocolate. Add crushed Oreos for some crunch.

Chocolate Chip Cookie Croissants

What happens when you combine chocolate chip cookies with croissants—two of the Internet's most beloved treats? Magic 🥰 The inside stays perfectly underbaked for that irresistible ooey-gooey center, while the outside gets golden and crisp. It's the kind of combo that'll live in your head rent-free.

SERVES 12

12 croissants
1 (16-ounce) package chocolate chip cookie dough

1. Preheat oven to 350°F. Line two large baking sheets with parchment paper.
2. Slice each croissant in half and stuff generously with cookie dough. Spread a little extra dough on top for good measure.
3. Place stuffed croissants on the prepared baking sheets and bake 10–12 minutes until the tops are golden and the cookie dough is just set. Serve warm.

Feeling adventurous? Swap out the chocolate chip cookie dough for other cookie dough flavors like peanut butter, sugar cookie, snickerdoodle, or *double* chocolate!

Deviled Strawberries

Everyone loves desserts that are as pretty as they are tasty. Enter Deviled Strawberries. This clever twist on deviled eggs combines juicy strawberries with a creamy, cheesecake-like filling, giving you all the indulgence without any fuss.

SERVES 10

2 tablespoons white vinegar
3 pounds large fresh strawberries
1 (8-ounce) package cream cheese, softened
1 cup confectioners' sugar
1 teaspoon vanilla extract
¾ cup heavy whipping cream
1 teaspoon lemon juice
¼ cup graham cracker crumbs

1. Fill a large bowl with 3 cups cold water. Stir in vinegar. Add strawberries and set aside to soak 5 minutes. Drain, rinse, and dry strawberries.
2. Cut strawberries in half lengthwise, then trim rounded sides so they sit flat. Use a small melon baller or spoon to carefully scoop out each middle. Set prepared strawberries on a parchment-lined baking sheet.
3. In a medium bowl, combine cream cheese, sugar, and vanilla. Using an electric mixer set to medium-high speed or a whisk, beat about 5 minutes until smooth. Add cream and beat on high speed 2–3 minutes until thick and firm. Gently stir in lemon juice until just combined.
4. Transfer filling to a piping bag fitted with a 1M star tip and refrigerate 10 minutes.
5. Pipe filling generously into each strawberry middle. Sprinkle lightly with graham cracker crumbs and serve immediately.

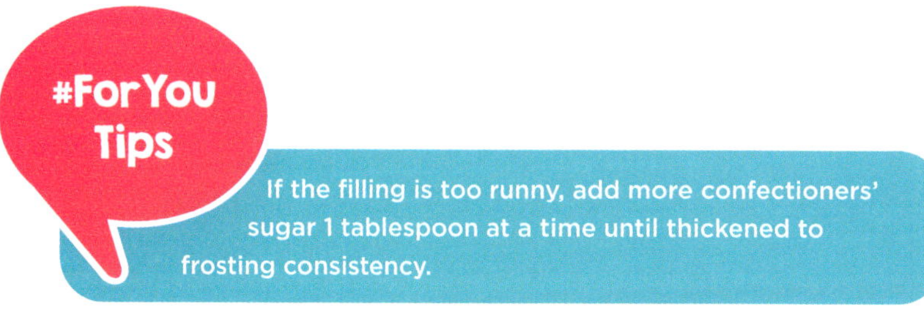

If the filling is too runny, add more confectioners' sugar 1 tablespoon at a time until thickened to frosting consistency.

Dragon's Beard

This delicate, hand-pulled candy has captivated people for centuries—going all the way back to the Han Dynasty in China! And now, it's having its viral moment. Dragon's Beard candy is sweet, airy, and totally unmatched in texture.

SERVES 4

2 cups granulated sugar
1 cup water
¼ cup corn syrup
½ teaspoon white vinegar
Food coloring
Cornstarch

1. In a large saucepan, combine sugar, water, corn syrup, and vinegar. Add food coloring drop by drop until the candy reaches your desired color. Stir briefly to blend the color, then heat over medium-high heat without stirring until mixture reaches 260°F.
2. Carefully pour mixture into a six-donut silicone mold, dividing mixture among all six molds. Set aside at room temperature until cool enough to handle.
3. Remove cooled candy from the mold and coat generously with cornstarch.
4. Start stretching and squeezing the candy gently into a large circle. Twist it into a figure eight, then bring both loops together and stretch again. Continue stretching, twisting, and doubling the number of loops, until it transforms into delicate, hair-thin strands.
5. If the candy starts to stick, dust with a little more cornstarch—but don't overdo it! Enjoy.

#ForYou Tips

Practice makes perfect! If the candy feels too stiff, warm it slightly with your hands to make it pliable again.

Whipped Lemonade

Lemonade is the ultimate summer refresher, but *Whipped* Lemonade? That's a whole new level of deliciousness. This creamy, tangy, and sweet treat exploded on social media for its unexpectedly smooth, dessert-like texture. It's almost like ice cream in a glass, and once you try it, you'll get the hype.

SERVES 2

2 cups ice
2 cups heavy cream
1 cup sweetened condensed milk
1 cup lemon juice (from about 5 lemons)
2 teaspoons vanilla extract
½ cup whipped cream
2 lemon wedges

1. In a blender, combine ice, heavy cream, condensed milk, lemon juice, and vanilla. Blend 1 minute at high speed until smooth and creamy.
2. Pour into two glasses and top each with whipped cream and lemon wedge.

TikTok Cinnamon Rolls

Cinnamon rolls just got a whole lot better thanks to some TikTok inspo. The secret? Heavy cream adds unbeatable richness, creating perfectly soft, gooey cinnamon rolls every time.

SERVES 10

Cinnamon Rolls

2 (17.5-ounce) cans Pillsbury Grands cinnamon rolls

1 cup heavy cream

½ cup (1 stick) unsalted butter, melted

1 tablespoon ground cinnamon

¾ cup light brown sugar

⅛ teaspoon salt

Cream Cheese Icing

1 (8-ounce) package cream cheese, softened

1 tablespoon unsalted butter, softened

1 teaspoon vanilla extract

1 tablespoon heavy cream

½ cup confectioners' sugar

1. Preheat oven to 350°F and grease a 9″ × 13″ baking dish.
2. Open cans of cinnamon rolls and set icing aside. Separate rolls and place them evenly spaced apart in prepared dish.
3. Pour cream over and around the cinnamon rolls, making sure each roll is fully coated.
4. In a small bowl, stir together melted butter, cinnamon, brown sugar, and salt. Spoon evenly over the top of each cinnamon roll.
5. Cover baking dish tightly with aluminum foil. Bake 30–35 minutes.
6. While rolls bake, prepare the Cream Cheese Icing. In a medium bowl, combine reserved icing, cream cheese, and softened butter. Using an electric mixer set to medium-high or a whisk, beat about 4 minutes until smooth. Add vanilla and cream, and beat again 1 minute. Gradually add confectioners' sugar, ¼ cup at a time, beating until fluffy and creamy.
7. Remove Cinnamon Rolls from oven, generously spread Cream Cheese Icing over tops of rolls, and serve warm.

S'mores Cookies

Cheese pull? Please. When it comes to dessert, it's all about the *marshmallow* pull! These cookies bring the cozy vibes of a campfire right to your kitchen, blending gooey marshmallow, melty chocolate, and soft, crumbly cookie perfection.

SERVES 12

1¼ cups all-purpose flour
½ teaspoon baking soda
½ cup granulated sugar
¾ cup light brown sugar
1 teaspoon salt
½ cup unsalted butter, softened
1 large egg
1 teaspoon vanilla extract
2 cups semisweet chocolate chips
6 graham crackers, each broken into 2 squares
4 (1.55-ounce) bars milk chocolate, each broken into 3 pieces
12 marshmallows

1. Sift flour and baking soda into a medium bowl and set aside.
2. In a large mixing bowl, combine granulated sugar, brown sugar, salt, and butter. Mix until smooth and creamy. Add egg and vanilla, and stir until light and fluffy. Fold in flour mixture, being careful not to overmix. Mix in chocolate chips.
3. Preheat oven to 350°F. Line a large baking sheet with parchment paper.
4. Arrange graham cracker squares in a single layer on prepared baking sheet. Place pieces of chocolate bars and marshmallows on top of each graham cracker.
5. Scoop a mound of cookie dough and flatten it into a disk with your hands. Press the disk over a graham cracker stack, fully covering marshmallows and chocolate.
6. Bake 12–15 minutes until the cookies are golden brown and slightly crisp on the edges.
7. Allow cookies to cool completely on the baking sheet before serving—this helps the marshmallow layer set for the ultimate gooey bite.

Dirty Soda

People are loving their sweet bubbly fix, and Dirty Soda has quickly become the Internet's obsession. Originating from Utah, this creamy concoction has a deliciously refreshing taste and *endless* flavor combos. Perfect for social hangs or a refreshing treat that totally fits with your self-care era, Dirty Soda is gonna be your new go-to drink for when you want something fun!

SERVES 1

1 (12-ounce) can Dr Pepper soda

2 tablespoons coconut coffee creamer

1 tablespoon sweet vanilla syrup

1. Fill a tall glass ½ full of ice and then add Dr Pepper.
2. Add creamer and syrup.
3. Stir gently to combine and enjoy immediately!

Can't find coconut creamer? Mix 1 tablespoon coconut syrup with 2 tablespoons heavy cream for a quick substitute.

Hot Cocoa Bombs

Hot Cocoa Bombs have exploded on social media. These festive, chocolaty delights are mesmerizing to watch burst open before your eyes. Simply place the bomb in a mug, pour 1–2 cups of hot whole milk over the top, stir, and you'll have a decadent cup of cocoa ready to sip 😋

SERVES 3

3 (4-ounce) bars semisweet baking chocolate, chopped
6 tablespoons hot cocoa powder mix
12 mini marshmallows
1 (4-ounce) bar white baking chocolate
3 peppermint candy canes, crushed

1. Place semisweet chocolate in the top of a double boiler or a heatproof bowl set over a pan of simmering water. Stir constantly until melted, being careful not to let the temperature exceed 90°F.
2. Carefully pour chocolate into six silicone half-sphere molds (about 2½" in diameter), filling halfway. Rotate molds gently to coat evenly, then invert molds and pour excess chocolate back into the bowl. Refrigerate molds 30 minutes or until set.
3. Gently remove chocolate shells from molds, placing them open-side up on a clean flat surface. Fill three chocolate shells with 2 tablespoons cocoa and 4 mini marshmallows each.
4. Warm a saucepan over medium-low heat about 2 minutes. Carefully place one of the remaining chocolate shells open-side down onto the warmed pan surface 2–5 seconds to slightly melt the edges. Quickly seal the warmed half onto a filled half-sphere, creating a complete chocolate sphere. Repeat with remaining chocolate shells. Refrigerate 30 minutes to allow chocolate to set.
5. In a small bowl, add white chocolate and microwave on high in intervals of 15–30 seconds, stirring after each, until just melted. Drizzle white chocolate over each Hot Cocoa Bomb and sprinkle with crushed peppermint candy.

Candied Cranberries

Maybe it's the magic of the holidays, but Candied Cranberries have become a must-try seasonal treat. Their tangy sweetness delivers a perfect pop of flavor, and they're easy to make (but impossible to resist). Whether you're snacking on them by the handful or sharing with friends, they're definitely gonna be a hit. These little bites of joy are the kind of treat that disappears as quickly as you set it out.

SERVES 4

2 cups fresh cranberries
1 cup orange juice
1 cup Sprite soda
1 cup confectioners' sugar

1. In a large plastic container with a lid, combine cranberries, orange juice, and Sprite. Ensure the cranberries are fully submerged. Cover and refrigerate 24 hours.
2. Preheat oven to 200°F. Line a large baking sheet with parchment paper.
3. Drain cranberries and place in a large bowl. Add sugar and toss until cranberries are evenly coated.
4. Spread coated cranberries on prepared baking sheet and bake 3–5 minutes, just enough to set the coating.
5. Refrigerate cranberries at least 1 hour. Serve and enjoy!

Honeycomb Candy

Move over, homemade sourdough—Honeycomb Candy is here! This viral kitchen experiment has captivated home cooks everywhere for its instant transformation from bubbling liquid to crisp, airy perfection.

SERVES 8

1¾ cups granulated sugar
¼ cup corn syrup
½ cup honey
½ cup water
½ teaspoon salt
1 teaspoon vanilla extract
2½ teaspoons baking soda
2 (4-ounce) bars semisweet baking chocolate, melted (optional)

1. Line a 9″ × 13″ baking dish with parchment paper and set aside.
2. In a large saucepan, stir together sugar, corn syrup, honey, water, salt, and vanilla. Heat over medium-high heat until mixture temperature reaches 300°F, swirling pan occasionally to prevent burning.
3. Remove pan from heat and quickly whisk in baking soda until mixture becomes light and foamy.
4. Immediately pour mixture into prepared pan. Do not spread or stir.
5. Allow candy to cool 3–4 hours until hardened.
6. Once set, remove candy from pan and break it into pieces with a knife.
7. If you like, drizzle candy with melted chocolate or dip pieces into the chocolate before serving.

Macaron Croissants

Croissants are already a star on their own, but enter the Macaron Croissant era, and you've got a viral masterpiece. This combo is as delicious as it is stunning—think light, fluffy croissants with a creamy pistachio filling and a crisp, macaron-style shell on top.

SERVES 6

3 large egg whites, room temperature
½ teaspoon cream of tartar
⅓ cup castor sugar
1 teaspoon vanilla extract
1 drop gel food coloring (optional)
1¼ cups almond flour
1½ cups confectioners' sugar
¼ teaspoon salt
6 croissants
1 (3.4-ounce) package instant pistachio pudding mix
1½ cups whole milk

1. Preheat oven to 300°F and line a large baking sheet with parchment paper.
2. In the bowl of a stand mixer, add egg whites and cream of tartar and beat at medium-high speed 30 seconds or until frothy. With the mixer running, gradually add castor sugar and continue beating about 3 minutes until stiff peaks form. Stir in vanilla and food coloring if using.
3. Sift flour, confectioners' sugar, and salt into a medium bowl. Gently fold flour mixture into egg white mixture until fully combined, creating a thick batter.
4. Place croissants on prepared baking sheet. Pipe macaron batter over tops of croissants, covering them evenly. Let dry 1 hour or until a skin forms on top.
5. Bake croissants 10–13 minutes until macaron topping is set and crisp. Transfer croissants to a wire rack and let cool completely.
6. In a medium bowl, whisk pudding mix with milk until thickened. Transfer to a piping bag with a metal tip. Poke the tip into the bottom of a croissant and pipe in the filling. Repeat with remaining filling and croissants. Enjoy!

Oreo Mug Cake

Late-night munchies hitting hard? The viral Oreo Mug Cake has your back. With just two ingredients and a microwave, you'll have a warm, sweet pick-me-up in minutes. It's like perfection in a mug—quick, easy, and *sooo* delicious.

SERVES 1

5 Oreo cookies
¼ cup whole milk

1. Place 4 Oreos in a microwave-safe mug. Pour in milk and mash with a fork until cookies break down and mixture forms a thick batter-like consistency.
2. Press remaining Oreo into the center of the batter.
3. Microwave on high 1 minute or until the cake is set.
4. Let cool slightly before digging in!

Mix It Up

Try experimenting with different Oreo flavors like churro, s'mores, cotton candy, cinnamon bun, or birthday cake, or even substitute other cookies like Chips Ahoy!, Biscoff, or Nutter Butter to create brand-new mug cakes!

Cinnamon Roll Donuts

Making donuts from scratch is tricky, but this shortcut hack brings you all the flavor, without the fuss 🔥 These viral Cinnamon Roll Donuts deliver golden, crispy perfection in just minutes—no yeast, no waiting. Whether they're for breakfast or a quick treat, this recipe is the easiest way to get that warm, sugary goodness—fast!

SERVES 6

½ cup granulated sugar
¾ teaspoon ground cinnamon
4 cups canola oil
1 (12.4-ounce) can Pillsbury cinnamon rolls

1. In a shallow dish, combine sugar and cinnamon. Set aside.
2. Heat oil in a large, deep pot over medium-high heat until it reaches 350°F.
3. Open can of cinnamon rolls and set icing aside. Separate rolls and flatten them slightly. Punch out a hole in the center of each roll to create a donut shape.
4. Fry donuts 2–3 minutes, flipping halfway through, until golden brown. Transfer to a wire rack to drain.
5. Let donuts cool 2–3 minutes, then dip in cinnamon sugar mixture to coat evenly.
6. In a small microwave-safe container, warm reserved icing for dipping or drizzling over the donuts and serve.

Standard US/Metric Measurement Conversions

VOLUME CONVERSIONS	
US Volume Measure	**Metric Equivalent**
⅛ teaspoon	0.5 milliliter
¼ teaspoon	1 milliliter
½ teaspoon	2 milliliters
1 teaspoon	5 milliliters
½ tablespoon	7 milliliters
1 tablespoon (3 teaspoons)	15 milliliters
2 tablespoons (1 fluid ounce)	30 milliliters
¼ cup (4 tablespoons)	60 milliliters
⅓ cup	90 milliliters
½ cup (4 fluid ounces)	125 milliliters
⅔ cup	160 milliliters
¾ cup (6 fluid ounces)	180 milliliters
1 cup (16 tablespoons)	250 milliliters
1 pint (2 cups)	500 milliliters
1 quart (4 cups)	1 liter (about)

WEIGHT CONVERSIONS	
US Weight Measure	**Metric Equivalent**
½ ounce	15 grams
1 ounce	30 grams
2 ounces	60 grams
3 ounces	85 grams
¼ pound (4 ounces)	115 grams
½ pound (8 ounces)	225 grams
¾ pound (12 ounces)	340 grams
1 pound (16 ounces)	454 grams

OVEN TEMPERATURE CONVERSIONS	
Degrees Fahrenheit	**Degrees Celsius**
200 degrees F	95 degrees C
250 degrees F	120 degrees C
275 degrees F	135 degrees C
300 degrees F	150 degrees C
325 degrees F	160 degrees C
350 degrees F	180 degrees C
375 degrees F	190 degrees C
400 degrees F	205 degrees C
425 degrees F	220 degrees C
450 degrees F	230 degrees C

BAKING PAN SIZES	
American	**Metric**
8 × 1½ inch round baking pan	20 × 4 cm cake tin
9 × 1½ inch round baking pan	23 × 3.5 cm cake tin
11 × 7 × 1½ inch baking pan	28 × 18 × 4 cm baking tin
13 × 9 × 2 inch baking pan	30 × 20 × 5 cm baking tin
2 quart rectangular baking dish	30 × 20 × 3 cm baking tin
15 × 10 × 2 inch baking pan	30 × 25 × 2 cm baking tin (Swiss roll tin)
9 inch pie plate	22 × 4 or 23 × 4 cm pie plate
7 or 8 inch springform pan	18 or 20 cm springform or loose bottom cake tin
9 × 5 × 3 inch loaf pan	23 × 13 × 7 cm or 2 lb narrow loaf or pate tin
1½ quart casserole	1.5 liter casserole
2 quart casserole	2 liter casserole

Index

C

D

E

F

G

H

I

J

K

L

M

N

O

P

Q

R

S

T

Author photo by Marc Cartwright Photography

Palestrina McCaffrey, better known as Little Remy Food on social media, is an amateur chef who brings her passion for food and love of learning to the kitchen. With her approachable style and honest feedback, she makes cooking fun and accessible for everyone. Known for testing viral recipes, she has become a trusted resource for home cooks looking to discover which recipes are genuinely worth re-creating. Discover more by following @littleremyfood on your favorite social media platforms.